FUN AND FANTASTICAL

HATS to KNIT

mary scott huff

Creative Publishing
international

Creative Publishing
international

First published in the United States of America by
Creative Publishing international, Inc., a member of
Quayside Publishing Group
400 First Avenue North, Suite 400
Minneapolis, MN 55401

1-800-328-3895
www.creativepub.com

Visit www.Craftside.Typepad.com for a behind-the-scenes
peek at our crafty world!

ISBN: 978-1-58923-794-0

Digital edition published in 2014
eISBN: 978-1-62788-005-3

10 9 8 7 6 5 4 3 2 1

Library of Congress Cataloging-in-Publication Data available

Technical Editor: Karen Frisa
Copy Editor: Karen Levy
Proofreader: Kari Cornell
Cover Design: Laura H. Couallier, Laura Herrmann Design
Book Design: Laura H. Couallier, Laura Herrmann Design
Illustrations: Mattie S. Wells
Photographs: Nancy J. S. Langdon

Printed in China

CONTENTS

Hatter: "Do you think I've gone round the bend?"

Alice: "I'm afraid so. You're mad, bonkers, completely off your head. But I'll tell you a secret. All the best people are."

—Lewis Carroll, *Alice's Adventures in Wonderland*

ιNTRODUCTION

THE FAMOUSLY OUTSPOKEN KNITTER ELIZABETH ZIMMERMANN
TELLS US IN HER BOOK, *Knitting Without Tears,* "PEOPLE WILL PUT
ANYTHING ON THEIR HEADS." I WOULD ADD TO THAT SENTIMENT THAT
PEOPLE WILL PUT ANYTHING ON THEIR HEADS, AS LONG AS IT'S REALLY
COZY, OR REALLY FABULOUS. THE CREATIONS IN THIS BOOK STRIVE TO
FULFILL BOTH OF THESE CRITERIA.

Knitted fabric is the perfect medium for fantastical hats because its properties lend themselves uniquely to each creation: warmth, stretch, softness.
Add to these the magical ability of knitting to be formed into almost any
shape with only simple increases and decreases. The equation is perfect:
Yarn + Idea + Knitting = Hat-sterpiece.

The projects that follow are fun to make, great to look at, and a delight to
give. But even more important, wearing them can transform you. Who will
you be today? A giant squid? A hedgehog? A flower fairy? Maybe all three!

In addition to knitting the patterns here, I hope you'll gain the confidence
to design your own creative knitted hats. It's easy to use the basic shapes
presented as springboards for brand-new inventions. Change the colors,
adjust the shaping in the ears or tentacles, or add whiskers or a snout
to create something uniquely your own. And of course, wear them with
aplomb. Remember, all the best hatters are really quite mad.

ARCHITEUTHIS

ARCHITEUTHIS ("ARCHIE" TO HIS FRIENDS) IS EXTREMELY POLITE, AS CEPHALOPODS GO. HE HARDLY EVER HOGS THE POPCORN AT THE MOVIES, OR FAILS TO RETURN HIS LIBRARY BOOKS ON TIME. ONE AFTERNOON, ARCHIE STUMBLED UPON AN ARTICLE IN *Doomed Voyages Quarterly* ABOUT A HORRIFIC SEA MONSTER NAMED KRAKKEN, WHO DRAGGED AN ENTIRE WHALING SHIP AND ITS CREW TO THE BOTTOM OF THE OCEAN AS A LATE-NIGHT SNACK. FEARING AN UNFAIR PUBLIC RELATIONS BACKLASH, ARCHIE IMMEDIATELY WROTE TO ME, USING SOME OF HIS FINEST INK.

"On behalf of all the ocean's well-behaved mollusks," wrote Archie, "I'd like to point out that only a rare few of us are murderous beasts. On the contrary, most of us do no harm to anyone, keeping a notoriously low profile. How else can you account for the fact that no one observed one of us in our own habitat until 2013?" Archie further asserted, "It's the ignorant folklore of the surface-dwellers that has impugned our character, not our actions or our eating habits. While I'm on the subject of meals, I'd like to remind everyone that it's the sperm whale who preys upon the giant squid, not the other way around. Accounts of whales with sucker scars and beak lacerations are widely exag-gerated. To those who spread such libelous rumors, I'd like to respond: You should see the other guy!"

I couldn't have put it any better myself. Here's to Archie, striking a blow for mild-mannered decency, beneath the waves and above.

Yarn

 Super Fine

Shown: Mighty Sock by Abstract Fiber, 50% superwash merino wool/50% Tencel, 3.5 oz (100 g)/ 382 yd (349 m): Sangria (MC), 2 skeins; Light Blue (CA) and Black (CB), oddments for eyes

Needles

Size 1 (2.25 mm) 16" (40 cm) circular

Size 2 (2.75 mm) 16" (40 cm) circular or size to obtain gauge

Size 2 (2.75 mm) set of dpn

Notions

Stitch markers

Tapestry needle

Hand sewing needle and thread

Wool roving or other stuffing

Plastic rings: thirty ½" (13 mm), twenty ⅝" (16 mm), fourteen ¾" (19 mm)

Gauge

29 sts and 34 rnds = 4" (10 cm) in St st on larger needle

Take time to check gauge

Sizes

Finished size: 16½ (18¾, 21)" (42 [47.5, 53.5] cm) circumference

MANTLE

With MC and smaller needle, CO 120 (136, 152) sts. Pm and join for working in rnds. Work in k1, p1 rib for ½" (1.25 cm). Change to larger needle. Knit every rnd until piece measures 4" (10 cm) from CO.

Next rnd: *K15 (17, 19), pm; rep from * to end of rnd.

Dec rnd: *Knit to 2 sts before marker, k2tog; rep from * to end of rnd—8 sts dec'd.

Rep dec rnd every other rnd 4 more times—80 (96, 112) sts. Rep dec rnd every 3rd rnd 5 times—40 (56, 72) sts. Rep dec rnd every 5th rnd 1 (3, 5) time(s)—32 sts. Rep dec rnd every 8th rnd 3 times—8 sts. Knit 7 rnds.

Dec rnd: *K2tog; rep from * to end of rnd—4 sts.

Knit 4 rnds. Break yarn and thread tail through rem sts. Fasten securely on WS.

Mantle Lining

Turn hat WS out. With MC, larger needle, and WS facing, pick up and knit 1 st in each purl bump in rnd below first dec rnd—120 (136, 152) sts. Pm and join for working in rnds.

Next rnd: *K15 (17, 19), pm; rep from * to end of rnd.

Dec rnd: *Knit to 2 sts before marker, k2tog; rep from * to end of rnd—8 sts dec'd.

Rep dec rnd every other rnd 4 (6, 8) more times—80 sts. Stuff top of hat, using chopstick or dpn to get stuffing into top point if needed. Rep dec rnd every other rnd 9 times—8 sts. Break yarn and thread tail through rem sts. Fasten securely on WS.

FLUKES (make 2)

With MC and larger needle, CO 80 sts. Pm and join for working in rnds. Knit 2 rnds.

Next rnd: K40, pm, k40.

Next rnd: K1, M1L, knit to 2 sts before marker, k2tog, ssk, knit to last st, M1R, k1.

Dec rnd: Knit to 2 sts before marker, k2tog, ssk, knit to end of rnd—2 sts dec'd.

Rep last 2 rnds 14 more times—50 sts.

Next rnd: K25, turn work WS out so RS are tog.

Arrange 25 sts on each of 2 dpn. Join sts using 3-needle BO (page 125). Turn fluke RS out. Stuff, then sew CO edges tog.

(continued)

ARMS (make 8)

With MC and larger dpn, CO 21 sts. Arrange 7 sts on each of 3 needles, pm, and join for working in rnds. Work even in St st until piece measures 6" (15 cm).

Dec rnd: [K2tog, knit to end of dpn] 3 times—3 sts dec'd.

Rep dec rnd every 16 rnds 3 more times—9 sts. Work 8 rnds, then rep dec rnd—6 sts. Work 8 rnds. Break yarn and thread tail through rem sts. Fasten securely on WS. Stuff with roving.

Tip: For easier stuffing, fold/roll over the top edge of the arm as many times as necessary to reach the narrow point. Use a chopstick or blunt double-pointed needle to get stuffing all the way into the point. Add stuffing a little at a time, unrolling the top of the arm as you go.

TENTACLES (make 2)

With MC, larger dpn, and using Judy's magic CO (page 124) or other toe-up method, CO 6 sts—3 sts on each of 2 dpn. Pm and join for working in rnds. Knit 2 rnds.

Inc rnd: K1, M1R, k1, M1L, k2, M1R, k1, M1L, k1—10 sts.

Knit 1 rnd.

Inc rnd: K1, M1R, k3, M1L, k2, M1R, k3, M1L, k1—14 sts.

Next rnd: K5, sl next 4 sts onto an empty dpn, k2 (of the 4 sl sts), pm, k7—5 sts on first and 3rd dpn, 4 sts on 2nd dpn.

Inc rnd: Knit to 1 st before marker, M1R, k1, sl marker, k1, M1L, knit to end of rnd—2 sts inc'd.

Next rnd: Knit.

Rep last 2 rnds 12 more times—40 sts.

Next short row (RS): K35, wrap & turn.

Next short row (WS): P30, wrap & turn. (See Short Rows, page 125)

Next short row: K25, wrap & turn.

Next short row: P20, wrap & turn.

Next short row: K15, wrap & turn.

Next short row: P10, wrap & turn.

Next short row: Knit to end of rnd, working wraps tog with wrapped sts.

Next rnd: Knit, working wraps tog with wrapped sts.

Knit 3 rnds.

Next short row (RS): K25, wrap & turn.

Next short row (WS): P10, wrap & turn.

Next short row: K10, knit wrap tog with wrapped st, k4, wrap & turn.

Next short row: P15, purl wrap tog with wrapped st, p4, wrap & turn.

Next short row: K20, knit wrap tog with wrapped st, k4, wrap & turn.

Next short row: P25, purl wrap tog with wrapped st, p4, wrap & turn.

Next short row: K30, knit wrap tog with wrapped st, knit to end of rnd.

Next rnd: K4, knit wrap tog with wrapped st, knit to end of rnd.

Add stuffing to end of piece before beg dec, and cont adding stuffing as you work dec.

Dec rnd: Knit to 2 sts before marker, k2tog, ssk, knit to end of rnd—2 sts dec'd.

Next rnd: Knit.

Rep last 2 rnds 13 more times—12 sts. Arrange sts evenly on 3 dpn and remove marker. Work 8 rnds even.

Inc rnd: [K1, M1L, knit to end of dpn] 3 times—3 sts inc'd.

Work 16 rnds even. Rep last 17 rnds 5 more times—30 sts. Work even until piece measures 4" (10 cm) from last inc rnd. BO. Stuff remaining length of tentacle with roving.

Tip: If you find stuffing forms clumps inside the narrow pieces, use a crochet hook to loosen and blend them.

EYES (make 2)

With CA and dpn, CO 64 sts. Pm and join for working in rnds.

Next rnd: *K8, pm; rep from * to end of rnd.

Dec rnd: *Knit to 2 sts before marker, k2tog; rep from * to end of rnd—8 sts dec'd.

Next rnd: Knit.

Rep last 2 rnds 5 more times—16 sts. Place 8 sts on each of 2 dpn. With RS tog, join sts using 3-needle BO.

Pupils (make 2)

With CB and dpn, CO 40 sts. Pm and join for working in rnds.

Next rnd: *K5, pm; rep from * to end of rnd.

Dec rnd: *Knit to 2 sts before marker, k2tog; rep from * to end of rnd—8 sts dec'd.

Next rnd: Knit.

Rep last 2 rnds 2 more times—16 sts. Place 8 sts on each of 2 dpn. With RS tog, join sts using 3-needle BO.

FINISHING

Sew flukes to each side of mantle invisibly by hand. Layer pupils on top of eyes and sew in place. Try on hat for eye placement and pin. Sew eyes in place. Sew plastic rings onto one side of each arm, beg at narrow end with 3 smallest rings, then 2 middle-size rings, then 1 largest ring, as shown. To curl ends of arms, thread a tapestry needle with MC. Knot yarn securely to narrow end of arm, on opposite side from rings. Make small running sts up one column of knit sts to desired length (the longer the line of running sts, the more curled each arm will be). Pull yarn snug to gather running sts and curl arm. Knot yarn securely through knitted fabric, and pull tails of gathering yarn to inside of piece. Sew rings to edge of each tentacle, beg at narrow end with 3 smallest rings, then 2 middle-size rings, then 3 largest rings, as shown. Sew top edges of arms and tentacles closed. Fold hat in half and mark center back with a pin. Pin 3 arms to each side of center back, then 1 tentacle, then rem arm. Sew in place at top and bottom of ribbed edge, as shown.

Attaching the Tentacles

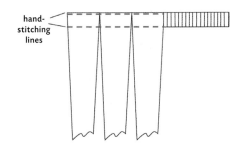

hand-stitching lines

bALDY

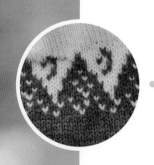

I HEAR THE EAGLE BIRD
WITH HIS GREAT FEATHERS SPREAD,
PULLING THE BLANKET BACK FROM
THE EAST,
HOW SWIFTLY HE FLIES,
BEARING THE SUN TO THE MORNING.

—Iroquois poem

Yarn

 Light

Shown: Cascade 220 Sport by Cascade Yarns, 100% Peruvian Highland wool, 1.75 oz (50 g)/164 yd (150 m): Walnut Heather #8013 (medium brown; CA), 1 skein; Natural #8010 (CB), 1 skein; Goldenrod #7827 (CC), 1 skein; Brown #8686 (dark brown; CD), 1 skein

Needles

Size 4 (3.5 mm) 16" (40 cm) circular or size to obtain gauge

Size 4 (3.5 mm) set of dpn

Notions

Stitch markers

Removable markers

Tapestry needle

Hand sewing needle and thread

Wool roving or other stuffing

Cardboard for tassels

Gauge

24 sts and 32 rnds = 4" (10 cm) in St st

Take time to check gauge

Sizes

Finished size: 18 (20, 22)" (45.5 [51, 56] cm) circumference

Stitch Guide

S2kp2: Sl 2 sts as if to k2tog, k1, p2sso—2 sts dec'd.

Stitch Pattern

BACK

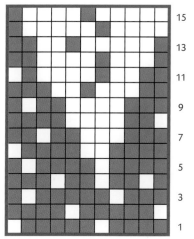

15
13
11
9
7
5
3
1

11-st rep

KEY

▨	CA
☐	CB

HAT

Back

With CA and circular needle, CO 55 (66, 77) sts. Work in k1, p1 rib for 3 rows. Work in St st until piece measures 2½ (3, 3½)" (6.5 [7.5, 9] cm) from CO, ending with a WS row. Work Rows 1–15 of Back chart once.

CROWN

Break CA. With CB, CO 53 (54, 55) sts onto same needle, pm, and join for working in rnds—108 (120, 132) sts total. Knit every rnd until piece measures 7 (7½, 8)" (18 [19, 20.5] cm) from CO for back.

Next rnd: K9 (12, 16), pm in next st, *k18 (20, 22), pm in next st; rep from * to last 9 (8, 6) sts, k9 (8, 6), remove marker, k0 (2, 5), pm for new beg of rnd—6 marked sts, 17 (19, 21) sts between marked sts.

Dec rnd: *Knit to 1 st before marked st, s2kp2; rep from * 5 more times, knit to end of rnd—12 sts dec'd.

Knit 2 rnds.

Rep last 3 rnds 7 (8, 9) more times—12 sts.

Next rnd: *K2tog; rep from * to end of rnd—6 sts.

Break yarn and thread tail through rem sts. Fasten securely on WS.

(continued)

Edging

With CA and RS facing, beg at lower right edge of back, pick up and knit 30 (33, 37) sts along right edge of back, 53 (54, 55) sts along crown CO sts, and 30 (33, 37) sts along left edge of back—113 (120, 129) sts total. Work 3 rows in k1, p1 rib. BO.

UPPER BEAK

With CC, dpn, and using Judy's magic CO (page 124) or other toe-up method, CO 8 sts —4 sts on each of 2 dpn. Pm and join for working in rnds.

Inc rnd: K1, M1R, knit to last st, M1L, k1—2 sts inc'd.

Next rnd: Knit.

Rep last 2 rnds 16 more times—42 sts.

Next short row (RS): K21, pm, knit to last 6 sts, wrap & turn. (See Short Rows, page 125)

Next short row (WS): Purl to last 6 sts, wrap & turn.

Next short row: Knit to 1 st before marker, M1R, k1, sl marker, k1, M1L, knit to last 12 sts, wrap & turn—44 sts.

Next short row: Purl to last 12 sts, wrap & turn.

Next short row: Knit to 1 st before marker, M1R, k1, sl marker, k1, M1L, knit to end of rnd, working wraps tog with wrapped sts—46 sts.

Knit 1 rnd, working wraps tog with wrapped sts. BO loosely.

LOWER BEAK

With CC, dpn, and using Judy's magic CO or other toe-up method, CO 8 sts —4 sts on each of 2 dpn. Pm and join for working in rnds. Knit 2 rnds.

Inc rnd: K1, M1R, knit to last st, M1L, k1—2 sts inc'd.

Next rnd: Knit.

Rep last 2 rnds 13 more times—36 sts. BO loosely.

EYES (make 2)

With CC, CO 17 sts. Work 2 rows in St st.

Next short row (RS): K16, wrap & turn.

Next short row (WS): P15, wrap & turn.

Next short row: K13, wrap & turn.

Next short row: P11, wrap & turn.

Next short row: K9, wrap & turn.

Next short row: P7, wrap & turn.

Next short row: Knit to end, working wraps tog with wrapped sts.

Next short row: Purl, working wraps tog with wrapped sts.

BO loosely.

Pupils (make 2)

With CD, CO 3 sts.

Next row (WS): P1, pm in next st, p2.

Knit 1 row. Purl 1 row.

Inc row (RS): Knit to marked st, M1R, k1, M1L, knit to end—2 sts inc'd.

Purl 1 row. Rep inc row—7 sts. Work 3 rows even.

Dec row (RS): Knit to 1 st before marked st, s2kp2, knit to end—2 sts dec'd.

Purl 1 row. Rep dec row—3 sts. Purl 1 row.

Next row (RS): S2kp2—1 st.

Next row: P1.

Break yarn and thread tail through rem st. Fasten securely on WS.

TASSELS (make 12)

Cut a piece of stiff cardboard 2½" (6.5 cm) wide. With CA, wrap cardboard 17 times; break yarn. Tie loops tog firmly at top edge of card. Cut tassel loops at bottom of card and remove card. With double strand of CA threaded on a tapestry needle, wrap tassel ¾" (2 cm) below top. Knot wrapping yarn and pull under wraps, cutting to same length as tassel. Trim ends evenly.

FINISHING

Weave in ends. Block hat and eye pieces (beak pieces look better unblocked). Stuff beak pieces. Center lower beak as shown and pin in place. Sew in place by hand. Place upper beak at center front as shown, with lower edge overlapping lower beak. Pin in place and sew. Tack upper and lower beak tog. Layer pupils over eyes and sew in place. Pin eyes in place at each side of beak and sew. With CD, embroider chain st (page 122) around eye and 1" (2.5 cm) past, as shown, to make eyebrow. Sew tassels along lower edge of back, spacing evenly.

bLUE CRAB

THE NATIONAL HARD CRAB DERBY IS HELD EVERY SUMMER IN CRISFIELD, MARYLAND, THE SELF-PROCLAIMED CRAB CAPITAL OF THE WORLD. AT THE DERBY, 50 CRABS ARE PLACED IN INDIVIDUAL SIDE-BY-SIDE COMPARTMENTS, LIKE RACE HORSES AT A STARTING GATE. WHEN THE RACE BEGINS, THE IMPRISONED CRABS RUSH OUT AND SCRAMBLE DOWN A SLANTED WOODEN PLATFORM THAT HAS BEEN DOUSED WITH WATER TO MAKE IT SLIPPERY.

The first crab that slides off the platform onto the ground is the winner of that heat. After many heats, the race concludes with all the winners of the previous heats clawing their way to the edge of the platform. One strong, perfect blue crab is proclaimed the year's winner of the Governor's cup race, named for Crisfield's native son, J. Millard Tawes, the 54th governor of Maryland. The owner of the champion crab receives a giant trophy, presented on stage by Miss Crustacean, winner of the festival beauty pageant. What the winning crab receives is anyone's guess. I like to think it's Amnesty from the Pot.

Yarn

 Fine

Shown: Alto by Abstract Fiber, 100% Blue Faced Leicester wool, 4.25 oz (120 g)/392 yd (358 m): Pacific (MC), 1 skein; Black (CA), 1 skein; White (CB), 1 skein

Needles

Size 3 (3.25 mm) 16" (40 cm) circular or size to obtain gauge

Size 3 (3.25 mm) set of 5 dpn

Notions

Stitch markers

Tapestry needle

Two ⅝" (16 mm) buttons (shown: La Petite #478)

6" (15 cm) square piece of wool felt or other backing material

½ yd (0.5 m) polyester boning

Wool roving or other stuffing

Hand sewing needle and thread

Gauge

28 sts and 38 rnds = 4" (10 cm) in St st

Take time to check gauge

Sizes

Finished size: 16 (18¼, 20½)" (40.5 [46.5, 52] cm) circumference

Notes

Less than 10 yd (9 m) are needed of CA and CB.

HELMET TOP

With MC and circular needle, CO 112 (128, 144) sts. Pm and join for working in rnds. Knit every rnd until piece measures 1½ (2, 2½)" (4 [5, 6.5] cm) from CO.

Next rnd: *K14 (16, 18), pm; rep from * to end of rnd.

Dec rnd: *Knit to 2 sts before marker, k2tog; rep from * to end of rnd—8 sts dec'd.

Next rnd: Knit.

Rep last 2 rnds 12 (14, 16) more times—8 sts. Break yarn and thread tail through rem sts. Fasten securely on WS.

SIDE

With MC and RS facing, pick up and knit 85 (97, 109) sts along helmet top CO edge (leaving a 27 [31, 35] st gap at end of row). Purl 1 row.

Dec row (RS): K2, ssk, knit to last 4 sts, k2tog, k2—2 sts dec'd.

Next row: Purl.

Rep last 2 rows 7 more times—69 (81, 93) sts. Work even until piece measures 3½ (4, 4½)" (9 [10, 11.5] cm) from pick-up row, ending with a WS row.

Shape lower left edge

Next short row (RS): K30, wrap & turn. (See Short Rows, page 125)

Next short row (WS): P30.

Next short row: K24, wrap & turn.

Next short row: P24.

Next short row: K18, wrap & turn.

Next short row: P18.

Next short row: K12, wrap & turn.

Next short row: P12.

Next short row: K6, wrap & turn.

Next short row: P6.

Left chin strap

Work back and forth on first 6 sts in St st until strap measures 2¼ (3¼, 3¾)" (5.5 [8.5, 9.5] cm), ending with a WS row.

Next row (RS): Ssk, k2, k2tog—4 sts.

Next row: P2tog 2 times—2 sts.

Next row: K2tog—1 st.

Break yarn and thread tail through rem st. Fasten securely on WS.

Shape lower right edge

With WS facing, rejoin MC to 63 (75, 87) side sts.

Next short row (WS): P30, wrap & turn.

Next short row (RS): K30.

Next short row: P24, wrap & turn.

Next short row: K24.

Next short row: P18, wrap & turn.

Next short row: K18.

Next short row: P12, wrap & turn.

Next short row: K12.

Next short row: P6, wrap & turn.

Next short row: K6.

Right chin strap

Work back and forth on last 6 sts in St st until strap measures ½ (1, 2)" (1.25 [2.5, 5] cm), ending with a WS row.

Buttonhole row (RS): K2, k2tog, yo, k2.

Work even until strap measures 2 (3, 3½)" (5 [7.5, 9] cm), ending with a WS row. Rep buttonhole row. Purl 1 row.

Next row (RS): Ssk, k2, k2tog—4 sts.

Next row: P2tog 2 times—2 sts.

Next row: K2tog—1 st.

Break yarn and thread tail through rem st. Fasten securely on WS.

LOWER EDGE

With MC, RS facing, and beg at end of left chin strap, pick up and knit 19 (21, 23) sts along side of strap, knit 57 (69, 81) side sts, working wraps tog with wrapped sts, then pick up and knit 19 (21, 23) sts along side of right strap, ending at end of strap—95 (111, 127) sts total. Work 2 rows in k1, p1 rib. BO in patt.

(continued)

OPENING EDGE

With MC, RS facing, and beg at end of right chin strap, pick up and knit 133 (153, 173) sts along right chin strap, side, helmet top CO edge, side, and left chin strap, ending at end of strap. Work 2 rows in k1, p1 rib. BO in patt.

Joining Claw Halves

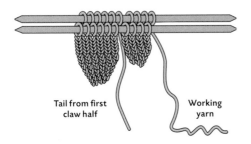

Tail from first claw half

Working yarn

CLAWS (make 2)

First half

With MC and using Judy's magic CO (page 124) or other toe-up method, CO 6 sts—3 sts on each of 2 dpn. Pm and join for working in rnds. Knit 2 rnds.

Inc rnd: K1, M1R, knit to last st, M1L, k1—2 sts inc'd.

Next rnd: Knit.

Rep last 2 rnds 4 more times—16 sts. Knit 2 rnds. Break MC and leave sts on 2 dpn.

Second half

With 2 more dpn, work as for first half, ending after working inc rnd and plain rnd 3 times—12 sts.

Join halves

Place second claw half on dpn with first claw half, as shown in illustration, leaving tail from first half hanging outside of piece—28 sts. Knit 3 rnds.

Next rnd: K14, pm, k14.

> **Tip:** You will be knitting the "arm" of the crab claw around the boning and stuffing. This is easier than trying to insert the stiffeners after the fact.

Cut a 6" (15 cm) length of boning and insert into longer side of claw, with curve of boning following curve of claw. Stuff claw.

Dec rnd: *K1, ssk, knit to 3 sts before marker, k2tog, k1; rep from * once more—4 sts dec'd.

Next rnd: Knit.

Rep last 2 rnds 3 more times—12 sts. Work even until piece measures 5" (12.5 cm) from tip of longer claw half.

Next rnd: [K1f&b] 12 times—24 sts.

Knit 2 rnds. BO loosely.

LEGS (make 8)

With MC, CO 12 sts. Distribute sts evenly onto 3 dpn, pm, and join for working in rnds.

First 2 legs only: Knit every rnd until piece measures ½" (1.25 cm).

Second 2 legs only: Knit every rnd until piece measures 1" (2.5 cm).

Third 2 legs only: Knit every rnd until piece measures 1½" (4 cm).

Fourth 2 legs only: Knit every rnd until piece measures 2" (5 cm).

All legs:

Dec rnd: *K2tog, knit to end of dpn; rep from * to end of rnd—3 sts dec'd.

Knit 4 rnds. Rep dec rnd—6 sts. Knit 4 rnds. Break yarn and thread tail through rem sts. Fasten securely on WS.

EYES (make 2)

With CA, CO 8 sts. Work 8 rows in St st. Break yarn, leaving a 12" (30.5 cm) tail. Thread tail through rem sts, then work running st around rem 3 sides. Place small ball of stuffing in center of square. Pull snugly on working yarn to gather sides around stuffing. Stitch securely to fasten. Pull tail to inside of eye and trim close to surface.

EYE STALKS (make 2)

With MC and dpn, CO 9 sts. Pm and join for working in rnds. Knit every rnd until piece measures 1" (2.5 cm).

Next rnd: [K1f&b] 9 times—18 sts.

Knit 2 rnds. BO loosely.

FINISHING

Sew edges of rib tog at ends of chin straps. Close gap between claw halves with yarn tail from first half. Weave in ends. Block helmet.

Claws

Insert more stuffing into arm if necessary. Thread a doubled length of MC on a tapestry needle. Sew a line of running sts from base of smaller claw half to end, through 1 column of knitted sts. Pull to gather slightly and cause arm to curve. Secure gathering strands. Pin claws in place at top of hat, as shown. Sew in place invisibly by hand. Cut 2 circles of felt backing material the same size as claw bases. Sew to underside of claws inside hat, tufting in centers, as shown.

Legs

Stuff legs. Sew legs in descending order of length at hat sides as shown.

Eyes

With hand sewing needle and thread, sew eyes to narrow end of eye stalks. With tapestry needle threaded with CB, embroider small circles as shown on tops of eyes. Stuff eye stalks. Try on hat for eye placement and pin. Sew eye stalks in place.

Sew buttons to left chin strap under buttonholes.

CALIFORNIA ROLL

SUSHI BY NUMBERS

Highest reported price ever paid for a tuna: $83,500, in 1992

Number of individual servings produced by the highest-priced tuna ever sold: 2,400

Length of longest sushi roll ever made, in feet: 4,381

Number of seconds it takes a bluefin tuna to accelerate from 0 to 50 mph: about 3

Number of seconds it takes a Porsche 911 GT3 to go from 0 to 50 mph: about 3

Number of seconds it takes an auctioneer at Tokyo's Tsukiji market to sell a tuna: about 3

Value of seafood moved through Tsukiji each day: $2.7 million

Number of sushi restaurants in Lexington, Kentucky: 1

Number of sushi restaurants in greater Los Angeles: 276

Number of rice balls a Tomoe MSR-3000 sushi machine makes in one hour: 3,000

Number of sushi pieces Masa Takayama of Manhattan's Masa makes in one hour: about 200

Price of a 12-piece sushi dinner at Randalls supermarket in Houston, Texas: $4.69

Price of an *omakase* dinner for one person at Los Angeles's Urasawa: $250

—*Food & Wine* magazine

Yarn

 Bulky

Shown: Tosh Chunky by Madelinetosh, 100% superwash merino wool, 3.5 oz (100 g)/165 yd (151 m): Antler #40 (cream; CA), 1 skein; Moorland #172 (dark green; CB), 1 skein; Butter #49 (yellow; CC), 1 skein; Afternoon #56 (pink; CD), 1 skein; Grasshopper #65 (light green; CE), 1 skein; Tomato #61 (orange; CF), 1 skein

Needles

Size 6 (4 mm) 16" (40 cm) circular

Size 7 (4.5 mm) 16" (40 cm) circular or size to obtain gauge

Size 7 (4.5 mm) set of dpn

Notions

Stitch markers

Tapestry needle

Hand sewing needle and thread

Gauge

20 sts and 30 rnds = 4" (10 cm) in St st on larger needle. Check gauge.

Sizes

Finished size: 18 (20, 22)" (45.5 [51, 56] cm) circumference

Notes

Only about 25 yd (23 m) are needed of CC, CD, CE, and CF.

Stitch Guide

Rice Stitch (multiple of 2 sts + 1)

Row 1 (RS): *K1tbl, p1; rep from * to last st, k1tbl.

Row 2: Knit.

Rep Rows 1 and 2 for patt.

CROWN

With CA and larger circular needle, CO 19 (21, 25) sts. Work 1 row in Rice st.

Inc row (WS): K1, M1R, work in Rice st to last st, M1L, k1—2 sts inc'd.

Rep last 2 rows 7 (8, 9) more times, working new sts into patt—35 (39, 45) sts. Work even until piece measures 3½ (4, 4½)" (9 [10, 11.5] cm) from CO, ending with a RS row.

Dec row (WS): K1, ssk, work in patt to last 3 sts, k2tog, k1—2 sts dec'd.

Rep dec row every WS row 7 (8, 9) more times—19 (21, 25) sts. BO.

Egg

With CC and larger circular needle, CO 12 sts.

Next row (RS): P1, k10, p1.

Next row (WS): K1, p10, k1.

Rep last 2 rows 4 more times. BO.

Crab

With CD and dpn, CO 32 sts. Pm and join for working in rnds. Knit 1 rnd.

Dec rnd: *K2, k2tog; rep from * to end of rnd—24 sts.

Knit 1 rnd.

Dec rnd: *K1, k2tog; rep from * to end of rnd—16 sts.

Knit 1 rnd. Arrange 8 sts on each of 2 dpn. With RS tog, join sts using 3-needle BO (page 125).

Avocado

With CE and larger dpn, CO 24 sts. Pm and join for working in rnds. Knit 1 rnd.

Dec rnd: *K2, k2tog; rep from * to end of rnd—18 sts.

Knit 1 rnd.

Dec rnd: *K1, k2tog; rep from * to end of rnd—12 sts.

Knit 1 rnd.

Dec rnd: *K2tog; rep from * to end of rnd—6 sts.

Break yarn and thread tail through rem sts. Fasten securely on WS.

Weave in ends and lightly steam all pieces to block. Arrange pieces as shown in center of crown and pin. Sew in place invisibly by hand with matching thread. With CB and a tapestry needle, embroider a chain st (page 122) around filling shapes as shown.

SIDE

With CB, smaller circular needle, and RS facing, pick up and knit 90 (100, 110) sts around edge of crown. Pm and join for working in rnds. Purl 1 rnd. Change to larger circular needle. Knit every rnd until piece measures 3 (3¼, 3½)" (7.5 [8.5, 9] cm) from pick-up rnd. Change to smaller needle. Purl 1 rnd for turning ridge. Knit 5 rnds. Fold hem to WS along turning ridge.

HEM

Join hem to side and BO as foll: Working in same column as next st on LH needle, pick up purl bump 5 rnds above turning ridge and place on LH needle, k2tog (purl bump and next st), *pick up next purl bump and place on LH needle, k2tog (purl bump and next st), pass 2nd st on RH needle over first to BO 1 st; rep from * to end of rnd.

FINISHING

Weave in ends. Steam lightly to block.

Tobico

With CF and a tapestry needle, embroider French knots (page 123) randomly as shown.

CHERRY PIE

THE ENGLISH PROCLIVITY FOR PIES MADE IT SAFELY ACROSS THE ATLANTIC, AND TOOK DEEP ROOT IN NEW ENGLAND. MARK TWAIN'S FRIEND CHARLES DUDLEY WARNER, WRITING IN 1872, FOUND THAT "ALL THE HILL AND COUNTRY TOWNS OF NEW ENGLAND ARE FULL OF THOSE EXCELLENT WOMEN, THE VERY SALT OF THE HOUSEKEEPING EARTH, WHO WOULD FEEL READY TO SINK IN MORTIFICATION THROUGH THEIR SCOURED KITCHEN FLOORS, IF VISITORS SHOULD CATCH THEM WITHOUT A PIE IN THE HOUSE. THE ABSENCE OF PIE WOULD BE MORE NOTICED THAN A SCARCITY OF BIBLE EVEN."

In 1902, the *New York Times* blasted a suggestion that pie should be eaten no more than twice a week. This, said the Times, was "utterly insufficient ... as anyone who knows the secret of our strength as a nation and the foundation of our industrial supremacy must admit. Pie is the American synonym of prosperity, and its varying contents the calendar of the changing seasons. Pie is the food of the heroic. No pie-eating people can ever be permanently vanquished."

Yarn

 Bulky

Tosh Chunky by Madelinetosh, 100% superwash merino wool, 3.5 oz (100 g)/ 165 yd (151 m): Winter Wheat #74 (MC), 1 skein; Tart (dark red; CA), 1 skein; Scarlet #80 (bright red; CB), 1 skein

Needles

Size 6 (4 mm) 16" (40 cm) circular

Size 7 (4.5 mm) 16" (40 cm) circular

Size 7 (4.5 mm) 24" (60 cm) circular or size to obtain gauge

Size 7 (4.5 mm) set of dpn

Notions

Stitch markers

Tapestry needle

Hand sewing needle and thread

Gauge

20 sts and 30 rnds = 4" (10 cm) in St st on larger needle

Take time to check gauge

Sizes

Finished size: 16 (19¼, 20¾)" (40.5 [49, 52.5] cm) circumference

BRIM

With CA and smaller needle, CO 80 (96, 104) sts. Pm and join for working in rnds. Knit 4 rnds. Purl 1 rnd for turning ridge. Change to larger needle. Knit 4 rnds. Change to MC. Fold CO edge to WS along turning ridge. Join hem as foll: *Working in same column as next st on LH needle, pick up CO st and place on LH needle, k2tog (CO st and next st); rep from * to end of rnd—80 (96, 104) sts.

SIDE

Knit 5 rnds.

Inc rnd: *K10 (12, 13), M1L; rep from * to end of rnd—88 (104, 112) sts.

Knit 5 rnds.

Inc rnd: *K11 (13, 14), M1L; rep from * to end of rnd—96 (112, 120) sts.

Work even in St st until piece measures 3½ (4, 4½)" (9 [10, 11.5] cm) from turning ridge. Purl 1 rnd.

CROWN

Change to CB.

Next rnd: *K12 (14, 15), pm; rep from * to end of rnd.

Dec rnd: *Knit to 2 sts before marker, k2tog; rep from * to end of rnd—8 sts dec'd.

Next rnd: Knit.

Rep last 2 rnds 10 (12, 13) more times, changing to dpn when necessary—8 sts. Break yarn and thread tail through rem sts. Fasten securely on WS.

Crust Ruffle

With MC and larger 16" (40 cm) circular needle, with crown facing and working along purl ridge at top of side, pick up and knit 96 (112, 120) sts around side. Knit 1 rnd.

Inc rnd: *K1f&b; rep from * to end of rnd—192 (224, 240) sts.

Knit 1 rnd. Change to 24" (60 cm) circular needle.

Inc rnd: *K2, k1f&b; rep from * to last 0 (2, 0) sts, k0 (2, 0)—256 (298, 320) sts.

Knit 2 rnds. Purl 1 rnd. BO.

Lattice (make 4)

With MC and larger circular needle, CO 30 (32, 34) sts. Work 2 rows in St st. BO.

Cherries
(make 25, or more if desired)

With CA and larger circular needle, CO 1 st.

Inc row: Knit into front, back, front, back, and front of st—5 sts.

Work 6 rows in St st, sl first st of every row.

Dec row: Pass 2nd, 3rd, 4th, and 5th st over first st—1 st.

Break yarn and thread CO tail through rem st. Pull snugly to form bobble and knot ends. Pull ends to inside of bobble and trim.

FINISHING

Weave in ends. Arrange lattice on crown as shown, weaving strips, and pin in place. Sew ends in place invisibly

by hand. Tack strips tog where they cross. Pin cherries to crown in spaces between lattice strips, as shown, and sew in place.

EARFLAPS

Try on hat and mark earflap locations. With CA, larger needle, and WS facing, pick up and purl 15 (17, 19) sts along turning ridge at base of brim at marked location.

Next row (RS): P1, *k1, p1; rep from * to end of row.

Cont in rib until piece measures 1 (1½, 2)" (2.5 [4, 5] cm) from pick-up row, ending with a WS row.

Dec row (RS): P1, ssk, work in rib to last 3 sts, k2tog, p1—2 sts dec'd.

Rep dec row every RS row 4 (5, 6) more times—5 sts. Work 5-st knitted cord until piece measures 14 (16, 18)" (35.5 [40.5, 45.5] cm) from pick up-row. Break yarn and thread tail through rem sts. Thread tail to inside of cord.

CROWN ROYAL

SOME OCCASIONS CALL FOR FORMAL WEAR. REALLY FORMAL WEAR. ROYAL CROWN JEWELERS BEING THIN ON THE GROUND AROUND HERE, WE (THE ROYAL WE, THAT IS) DECIDED TO KNIT OUR OWN.

How will Our subjects identify Us as their Sovereign without the proper headgear, after all? We especially like the ermine band around the bottom; a throne room can get chilly. We hardly need mention that sometimes a crown can be a heavy thing, so a bit of cushioning is always appreciated as well. You're welcome, all you other Majesties. Just one more service We provide.

Yarn

 Medium

Shown: Classic Wool Worsted by Patons, 100% wool, 3.5 oz (100 g)/210 yd (192 m): Royal Purple #00212 (MC), 1 skein; Yellow #77615 (CA), 1 skein; Cherry #77710 (CB), 1 skein; Emerald #77708 (CC), 1 skein; Royal Blue #77132 (CD), 1 skein

Moxie by Patons, 100% polyester, 3.5 oz (100 g)/96 yd (88 m): Lynx #81008 (CE), 1 skein; Dark Mink #81013 (CF), 1 skein

Needles

Size 8 (5 mm) 16" (40 cm) circular

Size 7 (4.5 mm) 16" (40 cm) circular or size to obtain gauge

Size 7 (4.5 mm) set of dpn

Size 3 (3.25 mm) straight or size to obtain gauge

Notions

Stitch markers	100-lb test monofilament fishing line
Removable markers	7 (8, 9) 2.5 mm jewelry crimp tubes
Tapestry needle	Jeweler's crimp pliers
Needle and thread	

Gauge

19 sts and 27 rnds = 4" (10 cm) in St st with MC on middle-size needle

13 sts and 16 rnds = 4" (10 cm) in St st with CE on middle-size needle

24 sts and 32 rows = 4" (10 cm) in St st with CA on smallest needle

Take time to check gauge

Sizes

Finished size: 18½ (20¼, 22)" (47 [51.5, 56] cm) circumference

Notes

Only about 15 yd (14 m) are needed of CB, CC, and CD.

Stitch Guide

S2kp2: Sl 2 sts as if to k2tog, k1, p2sso—2 sts dec'd.

CROWN

Fur band

With CA and larger circular needle, CO 60 (66, 72) sts. Pm and join for working in rnds.

Rnd 1: Knit.

Change to smaller circular needle.

Rnds 2–5: With CE, purl.

Rnds 6 and 7: *P4 with CE, p2 with CF; rep from * to end of rnd, stranding unused color loosely on WS.

Rnds 8–11: With CE, purl.

Rnds 12 and 13: With CA, knit.

Roll lower edge of fur band to WS and join CO edge to live sts as foll: *Working in same column as next st on LH needle, pick up CO st and place on LH needle, k2tog (CO st and next st); rep from * to end of rnd—60 (66, 72) sts.

(continued)

Tip: Yarn with a long "nap" (fuzzy strands) often looks better when purled, rather than knitted, because more strands are on the back side of each stitch than the front.

Gold band

Rnd 15: Knit, inc 28 (30, 32) sts evenly spaced—88 (96, 104) sts.

Rnd 16: Purl.

Rnds 17–21: Knit.

Rnd 22: Purl.

Crown

Change to MC and work even in St st until piece measures 2 (2½, 3)" (5 [6.5, 7.5] cm) from color change.

Next rnd: K5 (5, 6), pm in next st, *k11 (12, 13), pm in next st; rep from * 6 more times, k6 (7, 7)—8 marked sts, 10 (11, 12) sts between marked sts.

Dec rnd: *Knit to 1 st before marked st, s2kp2; rep from * 7 more times, knit to end of rnd—16 sts dec'd.

Next 2 rnds: Knit.

Rep last 3 rnds 4 (4, 5) more times—8 (16, 8) sts.

Next rnd: [K2tog] 0 (8, 0) times, knit to end of rnd—8 sts.

Break yarn and thread tail through rem sts. Fasten securely on WS.

Cross Pieces (make 2)

With CA, smallest needle, and using the long-tail method, CO 60 sts. Work 6 rows in St st, ending with a WS row. With RS facing, BO pwise.

Jewels

(make 12: 4 each with CB, CC, and CD)

With size 3 needles and leaving a 36" (91.5 cm) tail, CO 8 sts. Work 8 rows in St st. Break yarn, leaving a 12" (30.5 cm) tail. With tail threaded on a tapestry needle, run needle through sts on right side, bottom, and left side of rectangle, then through live sts, removing knitting needle. Pull gently on tail to gather sides of piece slightly. Wind CO tail into a ball and place in center of piece for stuffing. Pull snugly on working yarn to gather sides around stuffing. Stitch securely to fasten. Pull tail to inside of piece and trim close to surface.

Top Orb

With CA and size 3 needles, work as for jewels, but CO 10 sts and work 10 rows in St st.

FLEUR DE LIS (make 7 [8, 9])

With CA and size 3 needles, CO 5 sts.

Row 1 and all WS rows: Purl.

Row 2 (RS): K1, M1R, k1, yo, k1, yo, k1, M1L, k1—9 sts.

Rows 4, 6, 8, and 10: K3, yo, knit to last 3 sts, yo, k3—2 sts inc'd; 17 sts after Row 10.

Row 11 (WS): Purl.

Right point

Working over first 5 sts only, cont as foll:

Row 12 (RS): Ssk, k1, k2tog—3 sts.

Row 13 (WS): P3.

Row 14: S2kp2—1 st.

Break yarn and thread tail through rem st. Fasten securely on WS.

Center point

With RS facing, rejoin CA. Working over next 7 sts only, cont as foll:

Row 12 (RS): K3, yo, k1, yo, k3—9 sts.

Rows 14 and 16: K3, yo, knit to last 3 sts, yo, k3—2 sts inc'd; 13 sts after Row 16.

Row 18: Ssk, k1, yo, k2tog, k3, ssk, yo, k1, k2tog—11 sts.

Rows 20 and 22: Ssk, yo, k2tog, knit to last 4 sts, ssk, yo, k2tog—2 sts dec'd; 7 sts after Row 22.

Row 24: Ssk, yo, s2kp2, yo, k2tog—5 sts.

Row 26: K1, s2kp2, k1—3 sts.

Row 27 (WS): P3tog—1 st.

Break yarn and thread tail through rem st. Fasten securely on WS.

Left point

With RS facing, rejoin CA. Work as for right point.

FINISHING

Weave in ends. Block crown and ornament pieces.

Jewels

Pin jewels to gold band, spacing evenly and alternating colors as shown. Sew in place.

Cross pieces

Pin cross pieces to crown as shown, centered over dec lines. Sew to crown at ends.

Fleur de lis

To stiffen pieces, cut 7 (8, 9) pieces of monofilament, each 6" (15 cm) long. Bend each into a teardrop shape and place a crimp tube over both ends. Close crimp tube with crimping pliers to secure. Rep for all monofilament pieces. Tack each piece to WS of a fleur de lis as shown. Pin fleur de lis along top of gold band, spacing evenly. Sew to crown at lower edge and between points. Sew left and right points of adjacent fleur de lis tog.

Top orb

Sew in place at intersection of cross pieces as shown.

Finishing the Fleur de Lis

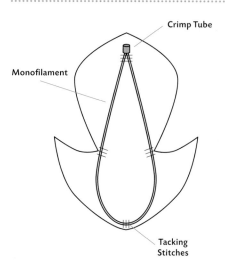

Crimp Tube

Monofilament

Tacking Stitches

ELFIN

The elves of the North Pole start out small, and they stay that way: their diet consists exclusively of sugar sprinkles, candy canes, and gumdrops. That's how they get so sweet. Baby elves play all day, because their parents are expert toymakers. They sleep all night, too, because they are dreaming about sugarplums. Of course it's chilly at the North Pole, so all  the little elves wear cozy hats, like this one.

Yarn

🧶**1** Super Fine

Shown: Socks That Rock Lightweight by Blue Moon Fiber Arts, 100% super-wash merino wool, 5.5 oz (155 g)/405 yd (370 m): Quilla (off-white; CA), 1 skein; Boysenberry (red-violet; CB), 1 skein; Brick (red; CC), 1 skein; Very Merry Green (green; CD), 1 skein; The New Color of Love (lime; CE), 1 skein; Nudie Patootie (tan; CF), 1 skein; Chest-nutty (brown; CG), 1 skein

Needles

Size 3 (3.25 mm) 16" (40 cm) circular or size to obtain gauge

Size 3 (3.25 mm) set of dpn

Notions

Stitch markers

Removable markers

Stitch holders

Waste yarn for provisional CO

Tapestry needle

Embroidery needle

Hand sewing needle and thread

Wool roving or other stuffing

Gauge

28 sts and 40 rnds = 4" (10 cm) in St st

Take time to check gauge

Sizes

Finished size: 16¼ (18½, 20¾)" (41.5 [47, 52.5] cm) circumference

Notes

Only about 25 yd (23 m) are needed of CF and about 1 yd (1 m) is needed of CG.

Stitch Guide

S2kp2: Sl 2 sts as if to k2tog, k1, p2sso—2 sts dec'd.

Stripe Pattern:

*4 rnds CA, 4 rnds CB, 4 rnds CC, 4 rnds CD, 4 rnds CE; rep from * as needed for stripe patt.

HELMET TOP

With CA, circular needle, and using a provisional CO method (page 124), CO 114 (130, 146) sts. Pm and join for working in rnds; beg of rnd is at center front of helmet. Working in stripe patt, cont as foll:

Next rnd: K15 (17, 19), pm, knit to last 12 (14, 16) sts, pm, knit to end of rnd.

Next rnd: S2kp2, knit to marker, sl marker, M1L, knit to marker, M1R, sl marker, knit to end of rnd.

Next rnd: Knit to last st, sl1p, remove marker, return sl st to LH needle, pm for new beg of rnd.

Rep last 2 rnds 8 more times.

Dec rnd: S2kp2, knit to end of rnd—2 sts dec'd.

Next rnd: Knit to last st, sl1p, remove marker, return sl st to LH needle, pm for new beg of rnd.

Rep last 2 rnds 2 more times—108 (124, 140) sts. Remove all markers except beg-of-rnd marker.

Next rnd: K1, pm in next st, *k27 (31, 35), pm in next st; rep from * 2 more times, knit to end of rnd—4 marked sts, 26 (30, 34) sts between marked sts.

Note: In foll section, shift beg-of-rnd marker as above before each dec rnd except first.

Dec rnd: S2kp2, *knit to 1 st before marked st, s2kp2; rep from * 2 more times, knit to end of rnd—8 sts dec'd.

Rep dec rnd every other rnd 3 (5, 7) more times—76 sts. Rep dec rnd every 4th rnd 4 times—44 sts. Rep dec rnd

Tip: Once you turn the work upside down to knit the sides, remember to reverse the order of the stripe progression. Also, color changes will happen at the beginning of wrong-side rows.

every 8th rnd 3 times—20 sts. Rep dec rnd every 16th rnd once—12 sts. Work 16 rnds even.

Dec rnd: [K2tog] 6 times—6 sts.

Break yarn and thread tail through rem sts. Fasten securely on WS.

HELMET BACK AND SIDES

Remove waste yarn from provisional CO and place sts onto circular needle. Place 18 (20, 22) sts on each side of center front st on holder—36 (40, 44) held sts; 78 (90, 102) sts on needle. With WS facing and beg with CE, join yarn to right front side of helmet. Purl 1 WS row.

Dec row (RS): K2, ssk, knit to last 4 sts, k2tog, k2—2 sts dec'd.

Next row: Purl.

Rep last 2 rows 5 more times—66 (78, 90) sts. Work even in patt until piece measures 1½ (2, 2½)" (4 [5, 6.5] cm) from last dec row, ending with a RS row.

(continued)

SHAPE RIGHT EARFLAP

Next row (WS): P23 (25, 27), place next 20 (28, 36) sts on holder for back neck, place foll 23 (25, 27) sts on holder for left earflap—23 (25, 27) sts for right earflap.

Dec row (RS): K2, ssk, knit to end of row—1 st dec'd.

Next row: Purl.

Rep last 2 rows 18 (20, 22) more times—4 sts. Complete all rows for current stripe. Pass 2nd, 3rd, and 4th st over first st. Break yarn and thread tail through rem st. Fasten securely on WS.

SHAPE LEFT EARFLAP

Place 23 (25, 27) left earflap sts onto needle. With WS facing, rejoin yarn. Purl 1 WS row.

Dec row (RS): Knit to last 4 sts, k2tog, k2—1 st dec'd.

Next row: Purl.

Rep last 2 rows 18 (20, 22) more times—4 sts. Complete all rows for current stripe. Pass 2nd, 3rd, and 4th st over first st. Break yarn and thread tail through rem st. Fasten securely on WS.

> **Tip:** Wait to weave in ends from color changes until all finishing steps are complete. Many ends will be hidden by those steps.

FRONT EDGING

Note: Edging is worked in a single color. With RS facing and CD, beg at tip of right earflap, pick up and knit 49 (55, 61) sts along right front edge,

k18 (20, 22) held sts, M1, k18 (20, 22) held sts, pick up and knit 49 (55, 61) sts along left front edge, ending at tip of left earflap—135 (151, 167) sts total. Purl 1 row. Pm in center front st.

Next row (RS): Knit to marked st, M1R, k1, M1L, knit to end of row—137 (153, 169) sts.

Purl 1 row.

Turning ridge (RS): Purl to 1 st before marked st, [p1f&b] 2 times, purl to end of row—139 (155, 171) sts.

Facing

Purl 1 WS row.

Dec row (RS): Knit to 2 sts before marked st, ssk, k1, k2tog, knit to end of row—2 sts dec'd.

Purl 1 row. Rep dec row—135 (151, 167) sts. Purl 1 row. BO. Trim yarn tails from color changes to 1" (2.5 cm). Turn hem to WS along turning ridge and pin in place, covering yarn tails. Sew in place invisibly by hand.

LOWER EDGING

Note: Edging is worked in a single color. With RS facing and CB, beg at end of front edging on left earflap, pick up and knit 36 (39, 42) sts along left earflap edge, k20 (28, 36) held sts, pick up and knit 36 (39, 42) sts along right earflap edge—92 (106, 120) sts total. Work 3 rows in St st, ending with a WS row. Purl 1 RS row for turning ridge.

Facing

Work 4 rows in St st, ending with a RS row. BO pwise. Turn hem to WS along turning ridge and pin in place. Sew invisibly by hand.

TOP LINING

With CA, WS of hat facing, and working along top of 2nd CA stripe above peak, pick up and knit 104 (120, 136) sts. Pm and join for working in rnds.

Next rnd: *K13 (15, 17), pm; rep from * to end of rnd.

Dec rnd: *Knit to 2 sts before marker, k2tog; rep from * to end of rnd—8 sts dec'd.

Rep dec rnd every other rnd 11 (13, 15) more times, adding stuffing when convenient—8 sts. Finish stuffing helmet. Break yarn and thread tail through rem sts. Fasten securely on inside of hat.

EARS (make 2)

With CF, dpn, and using Judy's magic CO (page 124) or other toe-up method, CO 16 sts—8 sts on each of 2 dpn. Pm and join for working in rnds.

Next rnd: K8, pm, k8.

Inc rnd: *K1, M1R, knit to 1 st before marker, M1L, k1; rep from * once more—4 sts inc'd.

Next rnd: Knit.

Rep last 2 rnds 2 more times—28 sts. Knit 8 rnds. Stuff piece lightly.

Dec rnd: *Ssk, knit to 2 sts before marker, k2tog; rep from * once more—4 sts dec'd.

Rep dec rnd every 3rd rnd 5 more times—4 sts.

Next rnd: [K2tog] 2 times—2 sts.

Next rnd: K2tog—1 st.

Break yarn and thread tail through rem st. Fasten securely on WS.

FINISHING

Weave in ends.

Top curl

Thread a tapestry needle with a double strand of CA. Fasten securely at top point of helmet. Sew a line of running sts through a single column of knitted sts for about 4" (10 cm). Pull snug to curl point down. Secure running sts and pull tail to inside of point.

Ears

With CG threaded on an embroidery needle, embroider swirls on ears with a backstitch (page 122) through both layers, "quilting" slightly, as shown. Pin ears at matching locations on each side of hat. Sew in place by hand.

fLOWER
FAIRY ··········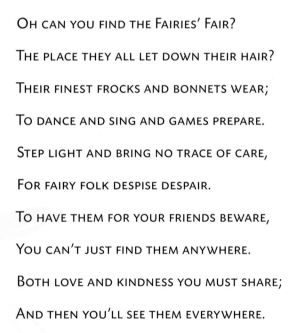

Oh can you find the Fairies' Fair?

The place they all let down their hair?

Their finest frocks and bonnets wear;

To dance and sing and games prepare.

Step light and bring no trace of care,

For fairy folk despise despair.

To have them for your friends beware,

You can't just find them anywhere.

Both love and kindness you must share;

And then you'll see them everywhere.

Yarn

 Fine

Shown: Ombré Sport Wool by Freia Fine, 100% wool, 2.64 oz (75 g)/217 yd (198 m): Amaranth, 1 skein

Needles

Size 5 (3.75 mm) 16" (40 cm) circular

Size 3 (3.25 mm) 16" (40 cm) circular or size to obtain gauge

Size 3 (3.25 mm) set of dpn

Notions

Stitch markers

Removable markers

Stitch holders

Tapestry needle

Hand sewing needle and thread

Wool roving or other stuffing

Small crochet hook

Gauge

28 sts and 44 rnds = 4" (10 cm) in St st on smaller needle. Take time to check gauge.

Sizes

Finished size: 16 (17¼, 18¼)" (40.5 [44, 46.5] cm) circumference

Stitch Guide

S2kp2: Sl 2 sts as if to k2tog, k1, p2sso—2 sts dec'd.

Notes

The largest size uses almost all of a skein of yarn. Consider purchasing a second skein as insurance. If a second skein is used, join as needed to maintain the color progression of the first skein.

COROLLA (Lower Petals)

With larger circular needle and beg at rose-colored end of skein, CO 162 (174, 186) sts. Pm and join for working in rnds.

Rnd 1: *K13 (14, 15), pm in next st, k14 (15, 16), pm on needle; rep from * to end of rnd.

Change to smaller circular needle.

Rnd 2: *K1, M1L, knit to 1 st before marked st, s2kp2, knit to marker, M1R, sl marker; rep from * to end of rnd.

Rnd 3: Knit.

Rnds 4–9: Rep Rnds 2 and 3.

Rnd 10: *K1, M1L, knit to 3 sts before marked st, ssk, s2kp2, k2tog, knit to marker, M1R, sl marker; rep from * to end of rnd—12 sts dec'd.

Rnds 11, 13, and 15: Rep Rnd 3.

Rnds 12, 14, and 16: Rep Rnd 10—114 (126, 138) sts after Rnd 16.

Work Rnd 3, then rep Rnds 2 and 3 until piece measures 4 (4½, 5)" (10 [11.5, 12.5] cm) from lowest point, ending with Rnd 3. Work [Rnd 10, Rnd 3, Rnd 2, Rnd 3] 5 (6, 7) times—54 sts. Work Rnd 10—42 sts.

Dec rnd: *Knit to 1 st before marked st, s2kp2, knit to marker; rep from * to end of rnd—12 sts dec'd.

Knit 1 rnd. Rep last 2 rnds—18 sts.

Next rnd: *K2tog; rep from * to end of rnd—9 sts.

Break yarn and thread tail through rem sts. Fasten securely on WS.

SEPAL (Upper Petals)

Petal (make 4)

With smaller needle and beg at deep purple end of skein, CO 2 sts.

Row 1 (WS): P2.

Row 2: K1f&b, k1—3 sts.

Row 3: P3.

Row 4: P1, M1R, knit to last st, M1L, p1—2 sts inc'd.

Row 5: K1, purl to last st, k1.

Row 6: P1, knit to last st, p1.

Row 7: Rep Row 5.

Rep Rows 4–7 8 more times—21 sts. Place sts on holder.

Join petals

With RS facing and smaller needle, work across all 4 petals, pm, and join for working in rnds—84 sts.

Base

Knit 6 rnds.

Next rnd: *K14, pm; rep from * to end of rnd.

Dec rnd: *Knit to 2 sts before marker, k2tog; rep from * to end of rnd—6 sts dec'd.

Rep dec rnd every 3rd rnd 10 more times—18 sts. Rep dec rnd every 5th rnd 2 times—6 sts. Work 6-st knitted I-cord until cord measures 2" (5 cm) from last dec rnd.

Dec rnd: K2tog, knit to end—5 sts.

Work 5-st knitted cord for 2" (5 cm).

(continued)

Dec rnd: K2tog, knit to end—4 sts.

Work 4-st knitted cord for 2" (5 cm).

Dec rnd: K2tog, knit to end—3 sts.

Work 3-st knitted cord for 1" (2.5 cm). Break yarn, leaving a 12" (30.5 cm) tail. Thread tail through rem sts. Fasten securely on WS.

LARGE LEAF

With smaller needle, CO 3 sts.

Next row (WS): K1, pm in next st, p1, k1.

Inc row (RS): P1, knit to marked st, M1R, k1, M1L, knit to last st, p1—2 sts inc'd.

Next row (WS): K1, purl to last st, k1.

Rep last 2 rows 2 more times—9 sts. Work 4 rows even.

Dec row (RS): P1, knit to 1 st before marked st, s2kp2, knit to last st, p1—2 sts dec'd.

Rep dec row every 4th row 2 more times—3 sts. Work 3 rows even.

Next row (RS): S2kp2—1 st.

Next row: P1.

Break yarn and thread tail through rem st. Fasten securely on WS.

SMALL LEAF (make 2)

With smaller needle, CO 3 sts.

Next row (WS): K1, pm in next st, p1, k1.

Inc row (RS): P1, knit to marked st, M1R, k1, M1L, knit to last st, p1—2 sts inc'd.

Next row (WS): K1, purl to last st, k1.

Rep last 2 rows 2 more times—9 sts. Work 2 rows even.

Dec row (RS): P1, knit to 1 st before marked st, s2kp2, knit to last st, p1—2 sts dec'd.

Rep dec row every RS row 2 more times—3 sts. Work 1 WS row.

Next row (RS): S2kp2—1 st.

Next row: P1.

Break yarn and thread tail through rem st. Fasten securely on WS.

BUDS (make 3)

With smaller needle and leaving a 12" (30.5 cm) tail, CO 6 sts. Work 6 rows in St st. Break yarn, leaving a 12" (30.5 cm) tail. Thread tail through rem sts, then work running st around rem 3 sides. Wind CO tail into a ball and place in center of piece for stuffing. Pull snugly on working yarn to gather sides around stuffing. Stitch securely to fasten. Pull tail to inside of bud and trim close to surface.

FINISHING

Weave in ends. Block pieces, allowing sepal petals to curl. Use crochet hook to pull small amounts of stuffing into cord at top of sepal. Thread a doubled length of yarn on a tapestry needle. Working from tip of cord, make running sts through a single column of knitted sts to base of cord. Pull snugly to curl cord and fasten securely on WS. Stuff sepal base. Layer sepal on top of corolla. Tack sepal to corolla invisibly with sewing thread all the way around. Layer buds and leaves as shown and sew in place.

fRILLY

THE ONLY MEMBER OF GENUS CHLAMYDOSAURUS, THE FRILL-NECKED LIZARD WAS DEPICTED ON THE REVERSE OF THE AUSTRALIAN TWO CENT COIN UNTIL 1991. INDIGENOUS TO THE NORTHERN REGIONS OF AUSTRALIA AND SOUTHERN NEW GUINEA, THE FRILL-NECKED LIZARD SPENDS MOST OF ITS TIME IN TREES, VENTURING TO THE GROUND ONLY TO HUNT FOR THE INSECTS AND SMALL RODENTS THAT MAKE UP ITS DIET. WHEN THREATENED, FRILLY OPENS HIS MOUTH WIDE AND EXTENDS THE COLORFUL RUFF AROUND HIS NECK. IF THAT DOESN'T WORK, HE RUNS FAST AND FAR AWAY FROM THREATS, NEVER STOPPING OR LOOKING BACK UNTIL REACHING SAFETY.

Our Frilly is a cozy balaclava, perfect for a day on the slopes or a chilly Halloween night. The helmet is made from solid yarn colors, while the frill gets its natural look from a coordinating long-repeat self-striping yarn. The points on the frill are stiffened with monofilament fishing line. Remember: If your frill doesn't scare your foe, run away.

Yarn

 Super Fine

Shown: 8/2 by Kauni, 100% wool, 5.25 oz (150 g)/656 yd (600 m): #RR green (MC), 1 skein; #EV green/rust variegated (CA), 1 skein; #AA white (CB), 1 skein

Needles

Size 3 (3.25 mm) 16" (40 cm) circular or size to obtain gauge

Size 3 (3.25 mm) set of dpn

Notions

Stitch markers

Removable markers

Stitch holders

Waste yarn for provisional CO

Tapestry needle

Hand sewing needle and thread

Wool roving or other stuffing

100-lb test monofilament fishing line

Twenty-eight 2.5 mm jewelry crimp tubes

Jeweler's crimp pliers
Permanent marking pens
Pins

Gauge

28 sts and 36 rnds = 4" (10 cm) in St st

Take time to check gauge

Sizes

Finished size: 16¼ (18, 21½)" (41.5 [45.5, 54.5] cm) circumference

Notes

Only about 20 yd (18 m) are needed of CB.

Stitch Guide

S2kp2: Sl 2 sts as if to k2tog, k1, p2sso—2 sts dec'd.

HELMET

With MC, CO 150 (162, 186) sts. Pm and join for working in rnds. Purl 1 rnd. Knit 1 rnd. Purl 1 rnd.

Next rnd: *K12 (13, 15), pm in next st, k13 (14, 16), pm on needle; rep from * to end of rnd.

Rnd 1: *K1, M1L, knit to 1 st before marked st, s2kp2, knit to marker, M1R, sl marker; rep from * to end of rnd.

Rnd 2: Knit.

Rnds 3–8: Rep Rnds 1 and 2.

Rnd 9: *Knit to 1 st before marked st, s2kp2; rep from * 5 more times, knit to end of rnd—12 sts dec'd.

Rnd 10: Knit.

Rep Rnds 1–10 twice more—114 (126, 150) sts. Remove all markers in sts except one (this will be center front), and remove all other markers except beg-of-rnd marker. Work even in St st until piece measures 5½ (5¾, 6)" (14 [14.5, 15] cm) from lowest point.

MOUTH

Next rnd: Knit to 2 sts after marked st, place last 3 sts on holder for mouth, work to end of rnd—111 (123, 147) sts.

Remove marker.

Next row (RS): Knit to held sts.

Work back and forth in rows, with mouth opening at beg and end of each row.

Next row (WS): Sl 1, purl to end of row.

Dec row (RS): Sl 1, ssk, knit to last 3 sts, k2tog, k1—2 sts dec'd.

Rep last 2 rows 22 more times—65 (77, 101) sts. With RS facing, transfer 1 st to LH needle, pm for beg of rnd, transfer st from LH needle to RH needle, CO 24 sts onto RH needle, pm for nose, CO 25 sts onto RH needle, join for working in rnds, k1, pm, knit to end of rnd—114 (126, 150) sts.

Rnd 1: Ssk, knit to marker, M1R, sl marker, k1, M1L, knit to 2 sts before marker, k2tog, knit to end of rnd.

Rnd 2: Knit.

Rnds 3–10: Rep Rnds 1 and 2.

Rnd 11: Pm in first st, knit to marker, remove marker, pm in next st, knit to 1 st before marker, pm in next st, k1, remove marker, k15 (18, 24), [pm in next st, k16 (19, 25)] 3 times.

Rnd 12: Knit to last st, sl1p, remove marker, transfer 1 st to LH needle, pm for new beg of rnd.

Rnd 13: *S2kp2, knit to 1 st before marked st; rep from * 5 more times, knit to end of rnd—12 sts dec'd.

Rnd 14: Knit to last st, sl1p, remove marker, transfer 1 st to LH needle, pm for new beg of rnd.

Rnds 15 and 16: Knit.

Rep Rnds 13–16 6 (8, 10) more times—30 (18, 18) sts.

Dec rnd: *K3tog (k2tog, k2tog); rep from * to end of rnd—10 (9, 9) sts.

Break yarn and thread tail through rem sts. Fasten securely on WS. Steam lightly to block, pinning as needed to make sharp points at lower edge.

(continued)

EYE BULGES
First bulge

With MC, CO 3 sts.

Row 1 (WS): P2, pm, p1.

Row 2: Knit to marker, M1R, sl marker, k1, M1L, knit to end of row—2 sts inc'd.

Row 3: Purl.

Rep Rows 2 and 3 8 (9, 10) more times—21 (23, 25) sts.

Next short row (RS): Knit to last 2 sts, wrap & turn. (See Short Rows, page 125)

Next short row (WS): Purl to last 2 sts, wrap & turn.

Next short row: Knit to last 4 sts, wrap & turn.

Next short row: Purl to last 4 sts, wrap & turn.

Next short row: Knit to last 6 sts, wrap & turn.

Next short row: Purl to last 6 sts, wrap & turn.

Next short row: Knit to end, working wraps tog with wrapped sts.

Next short row: Purl to end, working wraps tog with wrapped sts.

Next short row: Knit to last 6 sts, wrap & turn.

Next short row: Purl to last 6 sts, wrap & turn.

Next short row: Knit to last 4 sts, working wrap tog with wrapped st, wrap & turn.

Next short row: Purl to last 4 sts, working wrap tog with wrapped st, wrap & turn.

Next short row: Knit to last 2 sts, working wrap tog with wrapped st, wrap & turn.

Next short row: Purl to last 2 sts, working wrap tog with wrapped st, wrap & turn.

Next short row: Knit to end, working wrap tog with wrapped st.

Next short row: Purl to end, working wrap tog with wrapped st.

Next row (RS): K10 (11, 12), pm in next st, knit to end.

Next row: Purl.

Dec row (RS): Knit to 1 st before marked st, s2kp2, knit to end of row—2 sts dec'd.

Next row: Purl.

Rep last 2 rows 5 more times—9 (11, 13) sts. Place sts on dpn.

Second bulge

Work as for first bulge. Graft bulges tog.

EYES (make 2)

With yellow from CA skein, CO 3 sts.

Row 1 (WS): P1, pm in next st, p2.

Row 2: Knit to marked st, M1R, k1, M1L, knit to end of row—2 sts inc'd.

Row 3: Purl.

Rows 4–7: Rep Rows 2 and 3—9 sts.

Row 8: Knit.

Row 9: Purl.

Row 10: Knit to 1 st before marked st, s2kp2, knit to end of row—2 sts dec'd.

Row 11: Purl.

Rows 12 and 13: Rep Rows 10 and 11—5 sts.

Row 14: Rep Row 10—3 sts.

Row 15: P3tog—1 st.

Break yarn and thread tail through rem st. Fasten securely on WS. With dark brown from CA skein, embroider pupil onto eye with satin st (page 123) as shown.

LIPS

With orange from CA skein, dpn, and using a provisional method (page 124), CO 5 sts. Beg at corner of mouth, work 5-st attached cord around mouth, working held sts at center of lower edge, and grafting ends of cord tog.

UPPER TEETH

With CB, CO 54 sts. Work 6 rows in St st.

Picot row (RS): *P3tog, [yo] 2 times; rep from * to last 3 sts, p3tog—52 sts.

Next row (WS): *P1, (p1, k1) into double yo; rep from * to last st, p1.

Work 6 rows in St st. BO.

LOWER TEETH

With CB, CO 72 sts. Work as for upper teeth.

NOSE UNDERLINING

With MC, CO 3 sts.

Row 1 (WS): P1, pm in next st, p2.

Row 2: Knit to marked st, M1R, k1, M1L, knit to end of row—2 sts inc'd.

Row 3: Purl.

Rows 4–19: Rep Rows 2 and 3—21 sts.

Row 20: Knit.

Row 21: Purl.

Row 22: Knit to 1 st before marked st, s2kp2, knit to end of row—2 sts dec'd.

Row 23: Purl.

Rep Rows 22 and 23 7 more times, then work Row 22 once more—3 sts.

Next row (WS): P3tog—1 st.

Break yarn and thread tail through rem st. Fasten securely on WS.

(continued)

gARGOYLE

GARGOYLES IN ARCHITECTURE SERVE DUAL PURPOSES: THEY DIVERT BOTH RAINWATER AND EVIL SPIRITS. WHILE THIS ONE IS NO REPLACEMENT FOR A GOOD DOWNSPOUT, IT MIGHT STILL BE JUST THE THING FOR YOUR FAVORITE LITTLE MONSTER. AFTER ALL, EVERYBODY NEEDS TO LET THEIR HORNS SHOW NOW AND THEN.

Yarn

 Medium

Shown: Longwood by Cascade Yarns, 100% superwash extrafine merino wool, 3.5 oz (100 g)/191 yd (175 m): Lilac #27 (MC), 1 skein; Green Olive #15 (CA), 1 skein; Artisan Gold #08 (CB), 1 skein

Needles

Size 7 (4.5 mm) 16" (40 cm) circular or size to obtain gauge

Size 7 (4.5 mm) set of dpn

Notions

Stitch markers

Removable markers

Stitch holder

Waste yarn for provisional CO

Tapestry needle

Two ¾" (19 mm) buttons (shown: La Mode #43962)

Embroidery needle

Hand sewing needle and thread

Wool roving or other stuffing

Pins

Gauge

22 sts and 31 rnds = 4" (10 cm) in St st. Take time to check gauge.

Sizes

Finished size: 16 (19, 20¼)" (40.5 [48.5, 51.5] cm) circumference

Notes

Less than 10 yd (9 m) are needed of CB.

Stitch Guide

S2kp2: Sl 2 sts as if to k2tog, k1, p2sso—2 sts dec'd.

HELMET TOP

With MC and using a provisional CO method (page 124), CO 98 (114, 124) sts. Pm and join for working in rnds.

Next rnd: K16 (18, 20), pm in next st, knit to end of rnd. Note: Marked st is center front of helmet.

Dec rnd: Knit to 1 st before marker, s2kp2, knit to end of rnd—2 sts dec'd.

Next rnd: Knit.

Rep last 2 rnds 4 (4, 5) more times—88 (104, 112) sts.

Next rnd: Remove m, k2, pm for new beg of rnd, k20 (24, 26), pm in next st, *k11 (13, 14), pm in next st; rep from * 5 more times, k2—8 marked sts, 10 (12, 13) sts between marked sts.

Dec rnd: *Knit to 1 st before marker, s2kp2; rep from * to end of rnd—16 sts dec'd.

Next rnd: Knit.

Next rnd: Knit to end of rnd, remove marker, k1, pm for new beg of rnd.

Rep last 3 rnds 4 (5, 5) more times—8 (8, 16) sts.

Next rnd: [K2tog] 0 (0, 8) times, knit to end of rnd—8 sts.

Break yarn and thread tail through rem sts. Fasten securely on WS.

HELMET BACK AND SIDES

Remove waste yarn from provisional CO and place sts onto circular needle. Place 16 (18, 20) sts on each side of center front st on holder—32 (36, 40) held sts; 66 (78, 84) sts on needle. With WS facing, rejoin MC to right front side of helmet. Purl 1 WS row.

Dec row (RS): K2, ssk, knit to last 4 sts, k2tog, k2—2 sts dec'd.

Next row: Purl.

Rep last 2 rows 2 more times—60 (72, 78) sts. Work even in St st until piece measures 3 (3½, 4)" (7.5 [9, 10] cm) from last dec row, ending with a WS row.

SHAPE LEFT HELMET SIDE

Next short row (RS): K20, wrap & turn. (See Short Rows, page 125)

Next short row (WS): P20.

Next short row: K15, wrap & turn.

Next short row: P15.

Next short row: K10, wrap & turn.

Next short row: P10.

Next short row: K5, wrap & turn.

Next short row: P5.

(continued)

LEFT CHIN STRAP

Work back and forth on first 5 sts in St st until strap measures 3¼ (3¾, 4¼)" (8.5 [9.5, 11] cm), ending with a WS row.

Next row (RS): Ssk, k1, k2tog—3 sts.

Next row: P3.

Next row: S2kp2—1 st.

Break yarn and thread tail through rem st. Fasten securely on WS.

SHAPE RIGHT HELMET SIDE

With WS facing, rejoin MC.

Next short row (WS): P20, wrap & turn.

Next short row (RS): K20.

Next short row: P15, wrap & turn.

Next short row: K15.

Next short row: P10, wrap & turn.

Next short row: K10.

Next short row: P5, wrap & turn.

Next short row: K5.

RIGHT CHIN STRAP

Work back and forth on last 5 sts in St st until strap measures 1½ (2, 2½)" (4 [5, 6.5] cm), ending with a WS row.

Buttonhole row (RS): K1, k2tog, yo, k2.

Work even until strap measures 3 (3½, 4)" (7.5 [9, 10] cm), ending with a WS row. Rep buttonhole row. Purl 1 row.

Next row (RS): Ssk, k1, k2tog—3 sts.

Next row: P3.

Next row: S2kp2—1 st.

Break yarn and thread tail through rem st. Fasten securely on WS.

LOWER EDGE

With MC, RS facing, and beg at end of left chin strap, pick up and knit 23 (27, 31) sts along side of strap, knit 50 (62, 68) back neck sts, working wraps tog with wrapped sts, then pick up and knit 23 (27, 31) sts along side of right chin strap, ending at end of strap—96 (116, 130) sts total. Work 3 rows in k1, p1 rib. BO in patt.

OPENING EDGE

With MC, RS facing, and beg at end of right chin strap, pick up and knit 52 (60, 68) sts along right chin strap and side, knit 32 (36, 40) held sts at center front, pick up and knit 52 (60, 68) sts along side and left chin strap, ending at end of strap—136 (156, 176) sts total. Work 3 rows in k1, p1 rib. BO in patt.

WINGS (make 2)
Lower wing

With CA, CO 42 sts.

Next row: K13, pm in next st, k15, pm in next st, knit to end—2 marked sts, 14 sts at center between marked sts.

Knit 1 WS row.

Dec row (RS): *Knit to 1 st before marked st, s2kp2; rep from * once more, knit to end of row—4 sts dec'd.

Next row: Purl.

Rep last 2 rows 4 more times—22 sts. Knit 2 rows. Break yarn and leave sts on needle.

Upper edging

With CA, WS facing, and beg at lowest point of left selvedge edge, pick up and purl 6 sts along selvedge edge, p22, pick up and purl 6 sts along right selvedge edge—34 sts total. CO 4 sts. Work applied knitted cord over 34 sts. Cut 12 strands of CA, each about 6" (15 cm) long. Stuff knitted cord with these strands by threading 2 strands at a time through tapestry needle and pulling strands through knitted cord. Trim ends of stuffing strands and sew ends of cord closed.

HORNS (make 2)

With CA, CO 18 sts. Pm and join for working in rnds. Knit 6 rnds.

Next rnd: *K1, k2tog; rep from * to end of rnd—12 sts.

Knit 5 rnds.

Next rnd: [K2tog] 6 times—6 sts.

Knit 1 rnd. Break yarn and thread tail through rem sts. Fasten securely on WS.

EYES (make 2)

With CB and leaving an 18" (45.5 cm) tail, CO 8 sts. Work 8 rows in St st. Break yarn, leaving a 12" (30.5 cm) tail. Thread tail through rem sts, then work running st around rem 3 sides. Pull gently to partially gather sides of piece. Wind CO tail into a ball and place inside piece for stuffing. Pull snugly on working yarn to gather sides around stuffing. Sew securely to fasten. Pull working yarn tail to inside of eye and trim close to surface.

EYEBROWS (make 2)

With CA and dpn, CO 3 sts. Work knitted I-cord until piece measures 2½" (6.5 cm). Break yarn and thread tail through rem sts. Pull yarn tails to inside of cord.

FINISHING

Weave in ends. Steam helmet lightly to block, placing a pin at center front to create a sharp point. Stuff horns and pin to top of helmet, equidistant from center top and slightly forward. Sew in place by hand with matching thread.

With CA and embroidery needle, work satin st (page 123) pupil at center of eye. Pin one eye to base of each horn and sew in place. Pin one eyebrow to each eye and tack in place at center and ends. With CA and embroidery needle, work backstitch nostrils as shown at center front. With St st side of wings facing helmet, pin wings to each side of center back of helmet. Tack in place at center top and bottom of wings. Sew buttons to left chin strap under buttonholes.

GREEN MAN

Your eyes are dark as holly,
Of sycamore your horns,
Your bones are made of elder-branch,
Your teeth are made of thorns.
Your hat is made of ivy-leaf,
Of bark your dancing shoes,
And evergreen and green and green
Your jacket shirt and trews.
"Leave your house and leave your land
And throw away the key,
And never look behind," he creaked,
"And come and live with me."

—Charles Causley,
      "Green Man in the Garden"

67

Yarn

 Fine

Shown: Double Knitting by Jamieson's, 100% shetland wool, 0.88 oz (25 g)/82 yd (75 m): Moss #147 (dark yellow-green; MC), 4 skeins; Ivy #815 (olive green; CA), 1 skein; Leprechaun #259 (yellow-green; CB), 1 skein; Bracken #231 (yellow-brown; CC), 1 skein; Moorgrass #286 (blue-green; CD), 1 skein; Leaf #788 (dark green; CE), 1 skein

Needles

Size 3 (3.25 mm) 16" (40 cm) circular or size to obtain gauge

Size 3 (3.25 mm) set of dpn

Notions

Stitch markers

Stitch holder

Tapestry needle

Hand sewing needle and thread

Pins

Gauge

28 sts and 36 rnds = 4" (10 cm) in St st. Take time to check gauge

Sizes

Finished size: 18¼ (20½, 22¾)" (46.5 [52, 58] cm) circumference

Stitch Guide

S2kp2: Sl 2 sts as if to k2tog, k1, p2sso— 2 sts dec'd.

BALACLAVA

With MC and circular needle, CO 126 (140, 154) sts. Pm and join for working in rnds. Knit 1 rnd.

Next rnd: *K3, yo, k1, yo, k5, s2kp2, k2; rep from * to end of rnd.

Next rnd: Knit to end of rnd, remove marker, k1, pm for new beg of rnd.

Rep last 2 rnds until piece measures 3" (7.5 cm) from tip of points. Work in k1, p1 rib until piece measures 5" (12.5 cm) from tip of points.

Next rnd: Knit, inc 2 (4, 6) sts evenly spaced—128 (144, 160) sts.

Knit every rnd until piece measures 9 (9½, 10)" (23 [24, 25.5] cm) from tip of points.

Eye holes

BO 14 sts for left eye hole. Work back and forth over next 12 sts for eye separator as foll:

Next row (RS): K12, turn.

Next row: P12.

Dec row (RS): K1, ssk, knit to last 3 sts, k2tog, k1—2 sts dec'd.

Next row: Purl.

Rep last 2 rows 2 more times—6 sts. Work 2 rows in St st on these 6 sts. Work back and forth on these 6 sts as foll:

Inc row (RS): K1, M1R, knit to last st, M1L, k1—2 sts inc'd.

Next row: Purl.

Rep last 2 rows 2 more times—12 sts.

Break yarn and place 12 sts on holder. With RS facing, rejoin MC at base of right eye. BO 14 sts for right eye hole. Cont as foll, working back and forth in rows:

Next row (RS): Knit to end of rnd, turn.

Next row: Purl.

Dec row (RS): K1, ssk, knit last 3 sts of rnd, k2tog, k1—2 sts dec'd.

Next row: Purl.

Rep last 2 rows 2 more times—82 (98, 114) sts. Work 2 rows in St st.

Inc row (RS): K1, M1R, knit to last st of rnd, M1L, k1—2 sts inc'd.

Next row: Purl.

Rep last 2 rows 2 more times—88 (104, 120) sts. Knit to end of rnd.

Next rnd: Pm for beg of rnd, CO 14 sts over left eye, k12 held sts, CO 14 sts over right eye, join and work to end of rnd—128 (144, 160) sts.

Knit every rnd until piece measures 11 (11½, 12)" (28 [29, 30.5] cm) from tip of points.

Crown

Next rnd: *K16 (18, 20), pm; rep from * to end of rnd.

Dec rnd: *Knit to 2 sts before marker, k2tog; rep from * to end of rnd—8 sts dec'd.

Next rnd: Knit.

Rep last 2 rnds 14 (16, 18) more times—8 sts. Break yarn and thread tail through rem sts. Fasten securely on WS.

LARGE MAPLE LEAF (make 1)

With CA, CO 9 sts.

Row 1 (RS): K1, yo, k1, yo, k2, yo, k1, yo, k2, yo, k1, yo, k1—15 sts.

Row 2 and all WS rows: Purl.

Row 3: K2, yo, k1, yo, k4, yo, k1, yo, k4, yo, k1, yo, k2—21 sts.

Row 5: K3, yo, k1, yo, k6, yo, k1, yo, k6, yo, k1, yo, k3—27 sts.

Row 7: K4, yo, k1, yo, k8, yo, k1, yo, k8, yo, k1, yo, k4—33 sts.

Row 9: K5, yo, k1, yo, k10, yo, k1, yo, k10, yo, k1, yo, k5—39 sts.

Row 10 (WS): Purl.

(continued)

Right lobe

Working over first 13 sts only, cont as foll:

Rows 11 and 13: K13.

Row 15: K5, s2kp2, k5—11 sts.

Row 17: K4, s2kp2, k4—9 sts.

Row 19: K3, s2kp2, k3—7 sts.

Row 21: K2, s2kp2, k2—5 sts.

Row 23: K1, s2kp2, k1—3 sts.

Row 25: S2kp2—1 st.

Break yarn and thread tail through rem st. Fasten securely on WS.

Center lobe

With RS facing, rejoin CA. Working over next 13 sts only, cont as foll:

Row 11: K6, yo, k1, yo, k6—15 sts.

Row 13: K7, yo, k1, yo, k7—17 sts.

Rows 15 and 17: K17.

Row 19: K7, s2kp2, k7—15 sts.

Row 21: K6, s2kp2, k6—13 sts.

Row 23: K5, s2kp2, k5—11 sts.

Row 25: K4, s2kp2, k4—9 sts.

Row 27: K3, s2kp2, k3—7 sts.

Row 29: K2, s2kp2, k2—5 sts.

Row 31: K1, s2kp2, k1—3 sts.

Row 33: S2kp2—1 st.

Break yarn and thread tail through rem st. Fasten securely on WS.

Left lobe

With RS facing, rejoin CA. Working over last 13 sts, work as for right lobe.

Right corner lobe

With CA and RS facing, beg halfway down left edge of right lobe, pick up and knit 6 sts to base of lobe, 1 st at corner, and 6 sts up right edge of center lobe, ending one-third of way up lobe—13 sts total.

Row 1 and all WS rows: Purl.

Row 2: K5, s2kp2, k5—11 sts.

Row 4: K4, s2kp2, k4—9 sts.

Row 6: K3, s2kp2, k3—7 sts.

Row 8: K2, s2kp2, k2—5 sts.

Row 10: K1, s2kp2, k1—3 sts.

Row 12: S2kp2—1 st.

Break yarn and thread tail through rem st. Fasten securely on WS.

Left corner lobe

With CA and RS facing, beg two-thirds of way down left edge of center lobe, pick up and knit 6 sts to base of lobe, 1 st at corner, and 6 sts along right edge of left lobe, ending halfway up lobe—13 sts total. Work as for right corner lobe.

Fold CO edge in half and sew tog using CO tail.

SMALL MAPLE LEAF (make 1)

With CA, CO 9 sts.

Row 1 (RS): K1, yo, k1, yo, k2, yo, k1, k2, yo, k1, yo, k1—15 sts.

Row 2 and all WS rows: Purl.

Row 3: K2, yo, k1, yo, k4, yo, k1, yo, k4, yo, k1, yo, k2—21 sts.

Row 5: K3, yo, k1, yo, k6, yo, k1, yo, k6, yo, k1, yo, k3—27 sts.

Row 6 (WS): Purl.

Right lobe

Working over first 9 sts only, cont as foll:

Rows 7 and 9: K9.

Row 11: K3, s2kp2, k3—7 sts.

Row 13: K2, s2kp2, k2—5 sts.

Row 15: K1, s2kp2, k1—3 sts.

Row 17: S2kp2—1 st.

Break yarn and thread tail through rem st. Fasten securely on WS.

Center lobe

With RS facing, rejoin CA. Working over next 9 sts only, cont as foll:

Row 7: K4, yo, k1, yo, k4—11 sts.

Row 9: K5, yo, k1, yo, k5—13 sts.

Rows 11 and 13: K13.

Row 15: K5, s2kp2, k5—11 sts.

Row 17: K4, s2kp2, k4—9 sts.

Row 19: K3, s2kp2, k3—7 sts.

Row 21: K2, s2kp2, k2—5 sts.

Row 23: K1, s2kp2, k1—3 sts.

Row 25: S2kp2—1 st.

Break yarn and thread tail through rem st. Fasten securely on WS.

Left lobe

With RS facing, rejoin CA. Working over last 9 sts, work as for right lobe.

Right corner lobe

With CA and RS facing, beg two-thirds of way down left edge of right lobe, pick up and knit 4 sts to base of lobe,

1 st at corner, and 4 sts up right edge of center lobe, ending one-quarter of way up lobe—9 sts total.

Row 1 and all WS rows: Purl.

Row 2: K3, s2kp2, k3—7 sts.

Row 4: K2, s2kp2, k2—5 sts.

Row 6: K1, s2kp2, k1—3 sts.

Row 8: S2kp2—1 st.

Break yarn and thread tail through rem st. Fasten securely on WS.

Left corner lobe

With CA and RS facing, beg three-quarters of way down left edge of center lobe, pick up and knit 4 sts to base of lobe, 1 st at corner, and 4 sts up right edge of left lobe, ending one-third of way up lobe—9 sts total. Work as for right corner lobe.

Fold CO edge in half and sew tog using CO tail.

OAK LEAF (make 16: 4 each with CB, CC, CD, and CE)

CO 7 sts.

Row 1 (RS): K3, yo, k1, yo, k3—9 sts.

Row 2 and all WS rows except Rows 8, 14, and 20: Purl.

Rows 3 and 9: K3, yo, k3, yo, k3—11 sts.

Rows 5 and 11: K3, yo, k5, yo, k3—13 sts.

Rows 7 and 13: BO 3 sts, k3, yo, k1, yo, k6—12 sts.

Rows 8 and 14 (WS): BO 3 sts pwise, purl to end of row—9 sts.

Row 15: K3, yo, k3, yo, k3—11 sts.

Row 17: K3, yo, k5, yo, k3—13 sts.

Row 19: BO 4 sts, k2, yo, k1, yo, k6—11 sts.

Row 20 (WS): BO 4 sts pwise, purl to end of row—7 sts.

Row 21: Ssk, yo, s2kp2, yo, k2tog—5 sts.

Row 23: Ssk, k1, k2tog—3 sts.

Row 25: S2kp2—1 st.

Break yarn and thread tail through rem st. Fasten securely on WS. Fold CO edge in half and sew tog using CO tail.

MOUNTAIN ASH LEAF (make 5: 2 with CB, 1 with CC, and 2 with CD)

CO 3 sts.

Row 1 (RS): K1, yo, k1, yo, k1—5 sts.

Row 2 and all WS rows: Purl.

Row 3: K2, yo, k1, yo, k2—7 sts.

Row 5: Ssk, k1, yo, k1, yo, k1, k2tog.

Rep Row 5 every RS row 8 more times. Work 1 WS row.

Row 23: K2, s2kp2, k2—5 sts.

Row 25: K1, s2kp2, k1—3 sts.

Row 27: S2kp2—1 st.

Break yarn and thread tail through rem st. Fasten securely on WS.

BIRCH LEAF (make 4 with CA)

CO 3 sts.

Row 1 (RS): K1, yo, k1, yo, k1—5 sts.

Row 2 and all WS rows: Purl.

Row 3: K2, yo, k1, yo, k2—7 sts.

Row 5: K3, yo, k1, yo, k3—9 sts.

Rows 7 and 9: Knit.

Row 11: K3, s2kp2, k3—7 sts.

Row 13: K2, s2kp2, k2—5 sts.

Row 15: K1, s2kp2, k1—3 sts.

Row 17: S2kp2—1 st.

Break yarn and thread tail through rem st. Fasten securely on WS.

FINISHING

Weave in ends. Block balaclava and oak leaves, using pins to make sharp points (other leaves in sample were left unblocked). Pin all leaves to face as shown, overlapping edges. Tack leaves in place at centers and points with hand sewing needle and thread.

HEDGEHOG HELMET

THE COLLECTIVE NOUN FOR A GROUP OF HEDGEHOGS IS "PRICKLE." AS IN, "I KNIT AN ENTIRE PRICKLE OF HEDGEHOGS LAST WEEK." AND WHO WOULDN'T WANT TO WHEN THEY'RE SO MUCH FUN?

First make a simple cap, then pick up along its back edge and work down to form a helmet. Shape the neck edge with short rows, then continue out to the chin straps. Work a little ribbed edging all around, then the real fun begins: Pick up and knit your hedgehog's prickles with fur yarn! Stuff the inside and knit until the hedgehog's back is closed. Now make a cute little face, stuff, and stitch it on. Button eyes and nose finish the job. You won't be able to stop with one. And then you'll find yourself in quite a prickle.

Yarn

🧶**4** Medium, 🧶**5** Bulky

Shown: Fishermen's Wool by Lion Brand, 100% wool, 8 oz (227 g)/465 yd (425 m): Nature's Brown #150-126 (MC), 1 skein

Fun Fur Exotics by Lion Brand, 100% polyester, 1.75 oz (50 g)/55 yd (50 m): Tiger's Eye #320-125 (CA), 1 skein

Fun Fur by Lion Brand, 100% polyester, 1.75 oz (50 g)/64 yd (58 m): Champagne #320-124 (CB), 1 skein

Needles

Size 7 (4.5 mm) 16" (40 cm) circular or size to obtain gauge

Size 7 (4.5 mm) set of dpn

Size 5 (3.75 mm) 16" (40 cm) circular

Notions

Stitch markers

Removable markers

Tapestry needle

Two ½" (12 mm) buttons for eyes (shown: La Mode #29642)

One ⅝" (16 mm) button for nose (shown: La Petite #795)

Two ⅝" (16 mm) buttons for chin strap (shown: La Mode #3133)

Hand sewing needle and thread

Wool roving or other stuffing

Gauge

19 sts and 30 rnds = 4" (10 cm) in St st with MC on larger needle. Take time to check gauge

Sizes

Finished size: 16¾ (18½, 20¼, 23½)" (42.5 [47, 51.5, 59.5] cm) circumference

Stitch Guide

S2kp2: Sl 2 sts as if to k2tog, k1, p2sso—2 sts dec'd.

HELMET TOP

With MC and larger circular needle, CO 80 (88, 96, 112) sts. Pm and join for working in rnds. Work even in St st until piece measures 1½ (2, 2½, 3)" (4 [5, 6.5, 7.5] cm) from CO.

Next rnd: *K10 (11, 12, 14), pm; rep from * to end of rnd.

Dec rnd: *Knit to 2 sts before marker, k2tog; rep from * to end of rnd—8 sts dec'd.

Rep dec rnd every other rnd 8 (9, 10, 12) more times—8 sts. Break yarn and thread tail through rem sts. Fasten securely on WS.

LOWER HELMET

With MC, larger circular needle, and RS facing, pick up and knit 61 (65, 73, 85) sts along helmet top CO edge (leaving a 19 [23, 23, 27] st gap at end of row). Purl 1 row.

Dec row (RS): K1, ssk, knit to last 3 sts, k2tog, k1—2 sts dec'd.

Next row (WS): Purl.

Rep last 2 rows 7 (7, 9, 10) more times—45 (49, 53, 63) sts. Work even in St st until piece measures 4 (4½, 5, 5½)" (10 [11.5, 12.5, 14] cm) from pick-up row, ending with a WS row.

Shape lower left edge

Next short row (RS): K20, wrap & turn. (See Short Rows, page 125)

Next short row (WS): P20.

Next short row: K15, wrap & turn.

Next short row: P15.

Next short row: K10, wrap & turn.

Next short row: P10.

Next short row: K5, wrap & turn.

Next short row: P5.

Left chin strap

Work back and forth on first 5 sts in St st until strap measures 2¾ (3¼, 3¾, 4¼)" (7 [8.5, 9.5, 11] cm), ending with a WS row.

Next row (RS): K1, s2kp2, k1—3 sts.

Next row: P3tog—1 st.

Break yarn and thread tail through rem st. Fasten securely on WS.

Shape lower right edge

With WS facing, rejoin MC to 40 (44, 48, 58) lower helmet sts.

Next short row (WS): P20, wrap & turn.

Next short row (RS): K20.

Next short row: P15, wrap & turn.

Next short row: K15.

Next short row: P10, wrap & turn.

Next short row: K10.

Next short row: P5, wrap & turn.

Next short row: K5.

Right chin strap

Work back and forth on last 5 sts in St st until strap measures 1 (1½, 2, 2½)" (2.5 [4, 5, 6.5] cm), ending with a WS row.

Buttonhole row (RS): K2, yo, k2tog, k1.

Work even until strap measures 2½ (3, 3½, 4)" (6.5 [7.5, 9, 10] cm), ending with a WS row. Rep buttonhole row. Purl 1 row.

Next row (RS): K1, s2kp2, k1—3 sts.

Next row: P3tog—1 st.

Break yarn and thread tail through rem st. Fasten securely on WS.

(continued)

LOWER EDGE

With MC, smaller circular needle, RS facing, and beg at end of left chin strap, pick up and knit 20 (24, 26, 29) sts along side of strap, knit 35 (39, 43, 53) lower helmet sts, working wraps tog with wrapped sts, then pick up and knit 20 (24, 26, 29) sts along side of right strap, ending at end of strap—75 (87, 95, 111) sts total. Work 2 rows in k1, p1 rib. BO in patt.

OPENING EDGE

With MC, smaller needle, RS facing, and beg at end of right chin strap, pick up and knit 110 (126, 138, 158) sts along right chin strap, lower helmet, helmet top CO edge, lower helmet, and left chin strap, ending at end of strap. Work 2 rows in k1, p1 rib. BO in patt. Sew edges of rib tog at ends of chin straps. Weave in ends. Block helmet.

OUTER HELMET ("Spines")

With MC, larger circular needle, and RS facing, pick up and knit 80 (88, 96, 112) sts around helmet top, pm, and join for working in rnds.

With 1 strand of CA held tog with MC, work even in St st until piece measures 2 (2½, 3, 3½)" (5 [6.5, 7.5, 9] cm) from pick-up rnd.

Next rnd: *K10 (11, 12, 14), pm; rep from * to end of rnd.

Dec rnd: *Knit to 2 sts before marker, k2tog; rep from * to end of rnd—8 sts dec'd.

Rep dec rnd every other rnd 8 (9, 10, 12) more times, adding stuffing when convenient—8 sts. Finish stuffing helmet. Break yarn and thread tail through rem sts. Fasten securely on WS.

Tip: You may find that your hedgehog spines look better from the wrong side (purl side) of the fabric. If so, simply hold your work with the circle of knitting facing you, rather than away as you normally would (i.e., work wrong-side out). This puts the "wrong side" or purl side of the stockinette stitch on the outside of the helmet.

EYEBROWS (make 2)

With MC and larger circular needle, CO 20 sts.

Rows 1, 3, 5, and 7 (WS): Purl.

Row 2: K1, k2tog, *k2, k2tog; rep from * to last st, k1—15 sts.

Row 4: *K1, k2tog; rep from * to end of row—10 sts.

Row 6: *K2tog; rep from * to end of row—5 sts.

Row 8: K1, s2kp2, k1—3 sts.

Row 9: P3tog—1 st.

Break yarn and thread tail through rem st. Fasten securely on WS.

SNOUT

With MC, larger circular needle, and RS facing, pick up and knit 17 sts through straight edge of each eyebrow (34 sts total), then CO 26 sts—60 sts total. Pm and join for working in rnds. Knit 1 rnd.

Next rnd: K7, pm in next st, [k20, pm in next st] 2 times, k10, pm for new beg of rnd (remove old beg-of-rnd marker when you come to it)—3 marked sts, 19 sts between marked sts.

Dec rnd: *Knit to 1 st before marked st, s2kp2; rep from * 2 more times, knit to end of rnd—6 sts dec'd.

Rep dec rnd every 3rd rnd 5 more times—24 sts. Rep dec rnd every 5th rnd 2 times—12 sts. Knit 5 rnds. Break yarn and thread tail through rem sts. Fasten securely on WS.

EARS (make 2)

With MC and larger dpn, CO 16 sts. Pm and join for working in rnds.

Next rnd: K8, pm, k8.

Inc rnd: *K1, M1R, knit to 1 st before marker, M1L, k1; rep from * once more—4 sts inc'd.

Next rnd: Knit.

Rep last 2 rnds 3 more times—32 sts. Knit 3 rnds.

Dec rnd: *Ssk, knit to 2 sts before marker, k2tog; rep from * once more—4 sts dec'd.

Next rnd: Knit.

Rep last 2 rnds 3 more times—16 sts. Graft sts tog to close ear top.

FINISHING

Weave in ends. Block snout. Stuff snout. Pin in place at center front of helmet. Sew by hand. Fold each ear in half lengthwise and stitch at base to form pleat. Sew to helmet behind brows, as shown. Sew eye and nose buttons in place. With a double strand of CB threaded on a tapestry needle, embroider chain st (page 122) all around snout. Sew buttons to left chin strap under buttonholes.

JELLYFISH

HOW CAN ANYTHING AS DELICATE AS A JELLYFISH ALSO BE SO DANGEROUS? THEY ARE FLOATING UNDERWATER ENIGMAS: HUNDREDS OF TENTACLES, BUT ONLY ONE ORIFICE FOR NUTRITION, PROPULSION, PROCREATION, AND WASTE MANAGEMENT.

Jellyfish are clear as glass when you shine a light through them, but every color in the world in the darkness of the deep. Some are as small as 5 mm, while others are as large as 8 feet (7.2 m). Some varieties can swim as fast as 5 mph (8 km/h). Others glow in the dark. The speed and force with which a jelly delivers its sting is comparable to that of a bullet fired from a gun. Not bad for an organism that often doesn't even have eyes. Our hat version is fairly simple, too: a softly shaped beret worked from the decorative edging up to a series of spiraling open decreases, and finished with all the important jellyfish parts.

 Just remember to keep your tentacles to yourself.

Yarn

 Super Fine

Shown: Socks That Rock Lightweight by Blue Moon Fiber Arts, 100% superwash merino wool, 5.5 oz (155 g)/405 yd (370 m): Spot Rock One (MC), 1 skein; The New Color of Love (CC), 1 skein

Needles

Size 3 (3.25 mm) 16" (40 cm) circular or size to obtain gauge

Size 3 (3.25 mm) set of dpn

Size 2 (2.75 mm) 16" (40 cm) circular

Notions

Stitch markers

Tapestry needle

Size D/3 (3.25 mm) crochet hook

Hand sewing needle and thread

Elastic thread (optional)

Gauge

28 sts and 44 rnds = 4" (10 cm) in St st on larger needle. Take time to check gauge.

Sizes

Finished size: 16 (18¼, 20½)" (40.5 [46.5, 52] cm) circumference

BERET

Edging

With CC and larger circular needle, CO 224 (256, 288) sts. Pm and join for working in rnds.

Dec rnd: *K7, pass 2nd, 3rd, 4th, 5th, 6th, and 7th sts on RH needle over first st, yo, k1, yo; rep from * to end of rnd—112 (128, 144) sts.

Knit 1 rnd. Purl 1 rnd. Change to MC and smaller circular needle. Knit 1 rnd. Work in k1, p1 rib until rib measures 1" (2.5 cm).

Body

Change to larger circular needle.

Next rnd: *K1, k1f&b; rep from * to end of rnd—168 (192, 216) sts.

Knit every rnd until piece measures 3½ (4, 4½)" (9 [10, 11.5] cm) from top of rib.

SHAPE CROWN

Dec rnd: *K17 (20, 23), k2tog, yo, k2tog; rep from * to end of rnd—160 (184, 208) sts.

Next rnd: Knit.

Dec rnd: *Knit to 3 sts before yo 2 rnds below, k2tog, yo, k2tog; rep from * to end of rnd—8 sts dec'd.

Next rnd: Knit.

Rep last 2 rnds 16 (19, 22) more times —24 sts. Note: The spiral patt will approach the beg of rnd; move marker to the right as needed to keep it ahead of the spiral.

Dec rnd: *K1, k2tog; rep from * to end of rnd—16 sts.

Knit 1 rnd.

Dec rnd: [K2tog] 8 times—8 sts.

Knit 1 rnd. Break yarn and thread tail through rem sts. Fasten securely on WS.

Top Loops (make 4)

With CC and larger dpn, CO 4 sts. Work 4-st knitted I-cord, until piece measures 4" (10 cm) from CO. Break yarn and thread tail through sts. Weave in ends.

TENTACLES (make 10 [11, 12] with MC and 10 [11, 12] with CC)

Crochet a chain about 12" (30.5 cm) long. Fasten off.

FINISHING

Form a loop from each knitted cord and sew tog at ends. Sew all 4 loops tog at center and tack to top of beret as shown. Tack outer edges of loops to top of hat. Sew tentacles to lower inside edge of beret, as shown, alternating colors and leaving opening between tentacles at front.

Tip: When working with superwash yarns, ribbed areas can sometimes be less firm than needed. You can easily solve this problem by running a few rows of elastic thread under the knit stitches of the ribbing on the wrong side. Knot the ends of the thread together and weave in as you would yarn tails.

MEDUSA ···········

IT'S EASY TO BE MISUNDERSTOOD. GET CAUGHT WITH THE WRONG GUY (POSEIDON) IN THE WRONG PLACE (ATHENA'S TEMPLE), AND OF COURSE THERE'S GONNA BE TROUBLE.

Does having a permanent bad hair day really mean a girl is evil? And what about that stony gaze of hers? Sure, it may be taking the dirty look to a whole new level, but who among us hasn't wished someone would turn to stone (I'm looking at you, guy at the movies talking on your mobile phone)? For the record, I disagree with the stories that claim part of Medusa's punishment was to be alone for the rest of her life. Just look at all those adorable pets on her head!

Yarn

(4) Medium, (2) Fine

Shown: Shetland Heather by Jamieson's, 100% shetland wool, 1.75 oz (50 g)/101 yd (92 m): Amethyst #1310 (MC), 1 skein; Double Knitting by Jamieson's, 100% shetland wool, 0.88 oz (25 g)/82 yd (75 m): Scotch Broom #1160 (yellow; CA), 1 skein; Lavender #617 (light purple; CB), 1 skein; Anemone #616 (medium purple; CC), 1 skein; Violet #600 (dark purple; CD), 1 skein; Mint #770 (light green; CE), 1 skein; Jade #787 (medium green; CF), 1 skein; Tartan #800 (dark green; CG), 1 skein; Caspian #760 (light blue-green; CH), 1 skein; Lunar #680 (medium blue-green; CI), 1 skein; Petrol #750 (dark blue-green; CJ), 1 skein; China Blue #655 (light blue; CK), 1 skein; Lagoon #660 (medium blue; CL), 1 skein; Royal #700 (dark blue; CM), 1 skein; Scarlet #500 (red; CN), 1 skein; Celtic #790 (emerald green; CP), 1 skein

Needles

Size 10 (6 mm) 16" (40 cm) circular or size to obtain gauge

Size 10 (6 mm) set of dpn

Size 3 (3.25 mm) set of dpn or size to obtain gauge

Notions

Stitch markers

Removable markers

Tapestry needle

Hand sewing needle and thread

Wool roving or other stuffing

Approx 3 yd (3 m) polyester boning

Twenty-four 4 mm beads for eyes

Pins

Gauge

14 sts and 22 rnds = 4" (10 cm) in St st with MC on larger needle, before felting

28 sts and 36 rnds = 4" (10 cm) in St st with CB on smaller needle

Take time to check gauge

Sizes

Finished size: 18 (20, 22)" (45.5 [51, 56] cm) circumference

Stitch Guide

S2kp2: Sl 2 sts as if to k2tog, k1, p2sso—2 sts dec'd.

HAT
Side

With MC and circular needle, CO 72 (80, 88) sts. Pm and join for working in rnds. Work in St st until piece measures 3½ (4, 4½)" (9 [10, 11.5] cm) from CO.

Top

Next rnd: *K9 (10, 11), pm; rep from * to end of rnd.

Dec rnd: *Knit to 2 sts before marker, k2tog; rep from * to end of rnd—8 sts dec'd.

Next rnd: Knit.

Rep last 2 rnds 7 (8, 9) more times—8 sts. Break yarn and thread tail through rem sts. Fasten securely on WS.

Crown

Note: Crown is worked from the top down.

With 2 strands of CA held tog and larger circular needle, CO 96 (104, 112) sts. Pm and join for working in rnds.

Next rnd: K23 (25, 27), pm in next st, k48 (52, 56), pm in next st, knit to end—2 marked sts, 47 (51, 55) sts between marked sts.

Dec rnd: *Knit to 1 st before marked st, s2kp2; rep from * once more, knit to end of rnd—4 sts dec'd.

Next rnd: Knit.

Rep last 2 rnds 5 more times—72 (80, 88) sts. Work even in St st until piece measures 4 (4½, 5)" (10 [11.5, 12.5] cm) from tip of point. BO loosely.

SNAKES (make 12: 1 each with CB, CC, CD, CE, CF, CG, CH, CI, CJ, CK, CL, and CM)

Head

With smaller dpn and using Judy's magic CO (page 124) or other toe-up method, CO 8 sts—4 sts on each of 2 dpn. Pm and join for working in rnds.

Next rnd: K4, pm, k4.

Inc rnd: *K1, M1R, knit to 1 st before marker, M1L, k1; rep from * once more—4 sts inc'd.

Next rnd: Knit.

Rep last 2 rnds 3 more times—24 sts. Knit 8 rnds.

Dec rnd: *Ssk, knit to 2 sts before marker, k2tog; rep from * once more—4 sts dec'd.

Next rnd: Knit.

Rep last 2 rnds once more—16 sts.

Body

Knit every rnd until piece measures 9½" (24 cm) from CO.

Inc rnd: [K1f&b] 16 times—32 sts.

Knit 2 rnds. BO loosely.

(continued)

MERCURY

AMONG THE MANY MESSAGES CARRIED BY THE ROMAN GOD MERCURY WERE THE DREAMS OF MORPHEUS. POET OVID WROTE THAT MORPHEUS LIVED IN THE VALLEY OF SOMNUS, WHERE HE CREATED ALL THE DREAMS OF HUMANS.

Mercury was charged with delivering them, whenever people slept. Little wonder, then, that Mercury had to be quick. The patron saint of merchants and thieves, Mercury's influence stretches from the periodic table of the elements to modern-day superheroes. Wear this helmet, and think fast!

Yarn

 Medium

Shown: Classic Wool Worsted by Patons, 100% wool, 3.5 oz (100 g)/210 yd (192 m): Mercury #77044 (MC), 1 skein; Winter White #00201 (CC), 1 skein

Needles

Size 7 (4.5 mm) 16" (40 cm) circular or size to obtain gauge

Size 7 (4.5 mm) set of dpn

Size 4 (3.5 mm) set of dpn

Notions

Stitch markers

Stitch holders

Tapestry needle

Hand sewing needle and thread

Wool roving or other stuffing

Waste yarn for provisional CO and stitch holder

Pins

Gauge

22 sts and 28 rnds = 4" (10 cm) in St st on larger needle

24 sts and 32 rnds = 4" (10 cm) in St st on smaller needle

Take time to check gauge

Sizes

Finished size: 19 (20¼, 21¾)" (48.5 [51.5, 55] cm) circumference

HELMET
Brim

With MC, larger dpn, and using a provisional CO method (page 124), CO 12 sts. Pm and join for working in rnds. Work even in St st until piece measures 19 (20¼, 21¾)" (48.5 [51.5, 55] cm). Break yarn and place sts on waste yarn holder.

Side

With MC and circular needle, pick up and knit 104 (112, 120) sts through one column of knitted sts in brim. Pm and join for working in rnds. Work even in St st until piece measures 2 (2½, 2½)" (5 [6.5, 6.5] cm) from pick-up rnd.

Crown

Next rnd: *K13 (14, 15), pm; rep from * to end of rnd.

Dec rnd: *Knit to 2 sts before marker, k2tog; rep from * to end of rnd—8 sts dec'd.

Next rnd: Knit.

Rep last 2 rnds 11 (12, 13) more times —8 sts. Break yarn and thread tail through rem sts. Fasten securely on WS.

OUTER WINGS (make 2)

First wing tip: With CC, smaller dpn, and using Judy's magic CO (page 124) or other toe-up method, CO 6 sts— 3 sts on each of 2 dpn. Pm and join for working in rnds. Knit 2 rnds.

Inc rnd: K1, M1R, knit to last st, M1L, k1—2 sts inc'd.

Rep inc rnd every other rnd 2 more times—12 sts. Knit 4 rnds. Break yarn, leaving a 6" (15 cm) tail. Trim CO tail to 1" (2.5 cm). Remove marker. Place sts on holder.

Second wing tip: Work as for first tip, ending with 3 knit rnds rather than 4.

Third wing tip: Work as for first tip, ending with 2 knit rnds rather than 4.

Fourth wing tip: Work as for first tip, ending with 1 knit rnd rather than 4. Do not break yarn or place sts on holder.

Join tips: Arrange wing tips (from longest to shortest) on 2 dpn as shown. Knit across fronts of all 4 tips, then across backs—48 sts.

Joining Wing Tips

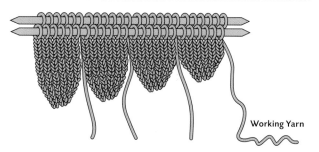

Working Yarn

Body of wing

Knit 3 rnds.

Next short row (RS): Knit to last 5 sts, wrap & turn.

Next short row (WS): Purl to last 5 sts, wrap & turn.

Next rnd: K19, pm, k19, knit wrap tog with wrapped st, k4. (Work rem wrap on foll rnd.)

Dec rnd: *K1, ssk, knit to 3 sts before marker, k2tog, k1; rep from * once more—4 sts dec'd.

Knit 2 rnds. Rep last 3 rnds 4 more times—28 sts.

Next short row (RS): Knit to 3 sts before marker, wrap & turn.

Next short row (WS): Purl to last 3 sts, wrap & turn.

Next short row: Knit to 6 sts before marker, wrap & turn.

Next short row: Purl to last 6 sts, wrap & turn.

Next rnd: Knit to end of rnd, working wraps tog with wrapped sts.

Next short row (RS): Knit to last 3 sts, working wraps tog with wrapped sts, wrap & turn.

Next short row (WS): Purl to 3 sts before marker, wrap & turn.

Next short row: Knit to last 6 sts, wrap & turn.

Next short row: Purl to 6 sts before marker, wrap & turn.

Next rnd: Knit to end of rnd, working wraps tog with wrapped sts.

Knit 1 rnd, working rem wraps. Graft sts tog to close end of wing. With yarn tails and tapestry needle, sew any gaps between wing tips closed, pulling tails to inside of wing.

FEATHERS (make 6)

With CC, smaller dpn, and using Judy's magic CO or other toe-up method, CO 6 sts—3 sts on each of 2 dpn. Pm and join for working in rnds. Knit 2 rnds.

Inc rnd: K1, M1R, knit to last st, M1L, k1—2 sts inc'd.

Rep inc rnd every other rnd 3 more times—14 sts.

First 2 feathers only: Knit every rnd until piece measures 4" (10 cm) from CO. BO.

Second 2 feathers only: Knit every rnd until piece measures 3½" (9 cm) from CO. BO.

Third 2 feathers only: Knit every rnd until piece measures 3" (7.5 cm) from CO. BO.

FINISHING

Block pieces. Stuff helmet brim. Remove provisional CO and graft CO sts to held sts of brim. Stuff feathers lightly. Sew feathers to WS of outer wings as shown. Try on helmet for wing placement and pin. Sew wings to helmet along entire curved edge, leaving wing tips free. Tack feathers to hat, leaving tips free.

RABBLE OF BUTTERFLIES

I'VE BEEN SWARMED. LUCKY FOR ME, THIS LOT IS PRETTY GOOD-NATURED. THERE'S MORE WHERE THEY CAME FROM, TOO. DID YOU KNOW THAT THE COLLECTIVE NOUN FOR BUTTERFLIES IS "RABBLE"? NO BETTER DESCRIPTION FOR AN UNRULY PROFUSION, IN MY OPINION. FURTHERMORE, A RABBLE-ROUSER IS A PERSON WHO SPEAKS WITH THE INTENT TO STIR THE PASSIONS OF HER AUDIENCE. JUST LIKE KNITTERS. HERE ARE A FEW YOU MAY HAVE HEARD MISQUOTED ELSEWHERE:

"Give me Free Patterns, or give me Death!" —*Patricia Henry*

"And so, my Fellow Knitters, ask not what yarn can do for you. Ask what you can do for yarn!" —*Jeanine Fitzsimmons Kennedy*

"I have a dream that one day on the red hills of Georgia the sons of knitters and the sons of crocheters will be able to sit down together at the table of brotherhood." —*Martina Louanne King*

"The only thing we have to fear is Moths, themselves!" —*Francis Delores Roosevelt*

"We shall defend our yarn stash, whatever the cost may be! We shall knit on the beaches, we shall knit on the landing grounds, we shall knit in the fields and in the streets, we shall knit in the hills; we shall never surrender." —*Winnifred Churchill*

STIRRING WORDS, AREN'T THEY? JUST MAKES ME WANNA GET OUT THERE AND START SOMETHING. Like a hat with butterflies.

Yarn

 Medium

Shown: Greenland by Cascade Yarns, 100% superwash merino wool, 3.5 oz (100 g)/137 yd (125 m): Burnt Orange #3530 (MC), 1 skein; Really Red #3513 (CA), 1 skein; Blue Hawaii #3518 (CB), 1 skein; Goldenrod #3531 (CC), 1 skein; Green Apple #3558 (CD), 1 skein; Nutmeg #3544 (CE), 1 skein

Needles

Size 6 (4 mm) 16" (40 cm) circular

Size 7 (4.5 mm) 16" (40 cm) circular or size to obtain gauge

Size 11 (8 mm) set of dpn

Notions

Stitch markers

Tapestry needle

¾ yd (0.7 m) ¼" (6 mm) polyester boning

Hand sewing needle and thread

Pins

Gauge

20 sts and 28 rnds = 4" (10 cm) in St st on larger circular needle

Take time to check gauge

Sizes

Finished size: 16 (19¼, 20¾)" (40.5 [49, 52.5] cm) circumference

HAT

Lower edge

With CA and small circular needle, CO 80 (96, 104) sts. Pm and join for working in rnds. Knit 5 rnds. Change to larger circular needle.

Picot rnd: *K2tog, yo; rep from * to end of rnd.

Knit 1 rnd. Change to MC. Knit 4 rnds. Fold CO edge to WS along picot rnd.

Join hem as foll: *Working in same column as next st on LH needle, pick up CO st and place on LH needle, k2tog (CO st and next st); rep from * to end of rnd—80 (96, 104) sts.

Side

Work even in St st until piece measures 1 (1¼, 1½)" (2.5 [3, 4] cm) from picot rnd.

Crown

Knit 1 rnd.

Dec rnd: *Knit to 2 sts before marker, k2tog; rep from * to end of rnd—8 sts dec'd.

Next rnd: Knit.

Rep last 2 rnds 10 (12, 13) more times —8 sts. Break yarn and thread tail through rem sts. Fasten securely on WS.

BUTTERFLIES (make 1 in CA, and 4 each in CB, CC, and CD)

Half wing

With dpn, CO 15 sts.

Row 1 (RS): P1, k13, p1.

Rows 2, 4, and 6: K1, purl to last st, k1.

Row 3: P1, ssk, k1, ssk, k1, M1R, k1, M1L, k1, k2tog, k1, k2tog, p1—13 sts.

Row 5: P1, [ssk] 2 times, k1, M1R, k1, M1L, k1, [k2tog] 2 times, p1—11 sts.

Row 7: P1, [ssk] 2 times, M1R, k1, M1L, [k2tog] 2 times, p1—9 sts.

Break yarn, leaving sts on needle. Make 2nd half wing to match, but do not break yarn. With RS tog, join half wings using 3-needle BO (page 125).

Bodies (make 13)

With CE and dpn, CO 4 sts. Work knitted I-cord, until piece measures 2½" (6.5 cm). Break yarn and thread tail through rem sts. Fasten securely on WS.

Antennae

Cut a 5" (12.5 cm) length of CE and thread on a tapestry needle. Thread yarn through end of body and remove needle. Tie ends in a square knot to fasten. Tie overhand knots in each end approx 1" (2.5 cm) from head and trim excess length close to knots.

FINISHING

Weave in ends. Block hat and wings. Working from WS, pin boning under purl ridge at top edge of hat, overlapping ends. Sew in place invisibly. Sew one body to each pair of wings invisibly by hand. Pin butterflies to hat as shown and tack in place by hand.

Next rnd: *K10 (12, 13), pm; rep from * to end of rnd.

Inc rnd: *Knit to marker, M1L, sl marker; rep from * to end of rnd—8 sts inc'd.

Work even until piece measures 2¼ (2½, 3)" (5.5 [6.5, 7.5] cm) from picot rnd. Rep inc rnd—96 (112, 120) sts. Work even until piece measures 3½ (3¾, 4)" (9 [9.5, 10] cm) from picot rnd. Purl 1 rnd.

SCOTTY ··········

SCOTTISH TERRIERS HAVE INSEAMS OF ABOUT 4" (10 CM) EACH, BUT BELIEVE THEMSELVES TO BE 10 FEET TALL. THEY ARE ABSOLUTELY FEARLESS, AND AS TENACIOUS AS, WELL, TERRIERS. BUT THAT'S NOT ALL THERE IS TO THE SCOT.

They are also clever, loyal, playful, and cuddly (but don't tell their enemies about that last one—they'll only deny it). My family is owned by both a black and a wheaten, who keep a careful watch on all our activities, in case anybody's behavior needs correction. The Scotties have very high standards for human supervision, notably the fetching of the treat box (must be conducted in a timely fashion) and the administration of walkies (must be performed at precise intervals). As long as we do things properly, the Scotties think people are just fine to live with. Especially when ear-scratching or belly-rubbing are called for.

Yarn

 Light

Shown: Socks That Rock Heavyweight by Blue Moon Fiber Arts, 100% superwash merino wool, 7 oz (198 g)/350 yd (320 m): Rauen (dark brown variegated; MC), 1 skein; Coral (CA), 1 skein; Chestnutty (brown; CB), 1 skein

Needles

Size 4 (3.5 mm) 16" (40 cm) circular or size to obtain gauge

Size 4 (3.5 mm) set of dpn

Notions

Stitch markers

Removable markers

Stitch holder

Waste yarn for provisional CO

Tapestry needle

Hand sewing needle and thread

Wool roving or other stuffing

3½" × 5" (9 × 12.5 cm) piece of cardboard

Gauge

24 sts and 32 rnds = 4" (10 cm) in St st

Take time to check gauge

Sizes

Finished size: 17¼ (20, 22¾)" (44 [51, 58] cm) circumference

Notes

Only about 30 yd (27 m) are needed of CA and CB.

Stitch Guide

S2kp2: Sl 2 sts as if to k2tog, k1, p2sso—2 sts dec'd.

HELMET TOP

With MC and using a provisional CO method (page 124), CO 104 (120, 136) sts. Pm and join for working in rnds. Knit every rnd until piece measures 2 (2½, 3)" (5 [6.5, 7.5] cm) from CO.

Next rnd: K12 (14, 16), pm in next st, *k13 (15, 17), pm in next st; rep from * 6 more times, k1—8 marked sts, 12 (14, 16) sts between marked sts.

Dec rnd: *Knit to 1 st before marker, s2kp2; rep from * to end of rnd—16 sts dec'd.

Next rnd: Knit.

Next rnd: Knit to end of rnd, remove marker, k1, pm for new beg of rnd.

Rep last 3 rnds 5 (6, 7) more times—8 sts. Break yarn and thread tail through rem sts. Fasten securely on WS.

HELMET BACK AND SIDES

Remove provisional CO; place 78 (90, 102) sts onto needle and 26 (30, 34) sts onto holder. With RS facing, join MC. Work back and forth in rows as foll:

Dec row (RS): K2, ssk, knit to last 4 sts, k2tog, k2—2 sts dec'd.

Next row: Purl.

Rep last 2 rows 4 more times—68 (80, 92) sts. Work even in St st until piece measures 2 (2½, 3)" (5 [6.5, 7.5] cm) from last dec row, ending with a WS row.

SHAPE LEFT EARFLAP

Short row 1 (RS): K24, wrap & turn. (See Short Rows, page 125)

Short row 2 (WS): P24.

Short row 3: K20, wrap & turn.

Short row 4: P20.

Short row 5: K16, wrap & turn.

Short row 6: P16.

Short row 7: K12, wrap & turn.

Short row 8: P12.

Short row 9: K8, wrap & turn.

Short row 10: P8.

Short row 11: K4, wrap & turn.

Short row 12: P4.

Next row (RS): Knit to end, working wraps tog with wrapped sts.

SHAPE RIGHT EARFLAP

Short row 1 (WS): P24, wrap & turn.

Short row 2 (RS): K24.

Short row 3: P20, wrap & turn.

Short row 4: K20.

Short row 5: P16, wrap & turn.

Short row 6: K16.

Short row 7: P12, wrap & turn.

Short row 8: K12.

Short row 9: P8, wrap & turn.

Short row 10: K8.

Short row 11: P4, wrap & turn.

Short row 12: K4.

Next row (WS): Purl to end, working wraps tog with wrapped sts.

Work 3 rows in k1, p1 rib. BO in patt.

OPENING EDGE

With RS facing, join MC to tip of right earflap. Pick up and knit 32 (35, 38) sts along earflap and front edge, knit 26 (30, 34) held sts, pick up and knit 32 (35, 38) sts along front and left earflap edge—90 (100, 110) sts total. Work 3 rows in k1, p1 rib. BO in patt.

MUZZLE

With MC and dpn, CO 48 sts. Arrange sts evenly on dpn and join for working in rnds. Knit every rnd until piece measures 1½" (4 cm) from CO.

Next rnd: *K8, pm; rep from * to end of rnd.

Dec rnd: *Knit to 2 sts before marker, k2tog; rep from * to end of rnd—6 sts dec'd.

Knit 3 rnds. Rep last 4 rnds 2 more times—30 sts.

Dec rnd: *Knit to 3 sts before marker, k3tog; rep from * to end of rnd—12 sts dec'd.

Next rnd: Knit.

Rep last 2 rnds once more—6 sts. Break yarn and thread tail through rem sts. Fasten securely on WS.

(continued)

EARS (make 2)

With MC and dpn, CO 30 sts. Arrange sts evenly on dpn and join for working in rnds. Knit every rnd until piece measures 1" (2.5 cm) from CO.

Next rnd: K15, pm, k15.

Dec rnd: *Ssk, knit to 2 sts before marker, k2tog; rep from * once more —4 sts dec'd.

Rep dec rnd every 4th rnd 2 more times—18 sts. Rep dec rnd every other rnd 3 times—6 sts.

Dec rnd: [S2kp2] 2 times—2 sts.

Break yarn and thread tail through rem sts. Fasten securely on WS.

Ear Lining (make 2)

With CA, CO 13 sts. Work 4 rows in St st, sl first st of every row.

Dec row (RS): Sl 1, ssk, knit to last 3 sts, k2tog, k1—2 sts dec'd.

Rep dec row every 4th row 2 more times—7 sts. Rep dec row every other row once—5 sts. Work 1 WS row.

Dec row (RS): Sl 1, s2kp2, k1—3 sts.

Next row (WS): Sl 1, p2.

Next row: S2kp2—1 st.

Break yarn and thread tail through rem st. Fasten securely on WS.

TONGUE

With CA and using Judy's magic CO (page 124) or other toe-up method, CO 8 sts—4 sts on each of 2 dpn. Pm and join for working in rnds.

Next rnd: K4, pm, k4.

Inc rnd: *K1, M1R, knit to 1 st before marker, M1L, k1; rep from * once more—4 sts inc'd.

Next rnd: Knit.

Rep last 2 rnds once more—16 sts. Knit 5 rnds. Arrange sts evenly on 2 dpn. With WS tog, join sts using 3-needle BO (page 125).

NOSE

With CB, CO 20 sts. Pm and join for working in rnds. Knit 5 rnds.

Next rnd: [K2tog] 10 times—10 sts.

Knit 1 rnd.

Next rnd: [K2tog] 5 times—5 sts.

Break yarn and thread tail through rem sts. Fasten securely on WS.

EYES (make 2)

With CB and leaving an 18" (45.5 cm) tail, CO 10 sts. Work 9 rows in St st. Break yarn, leaving a 12" (30.5 cm) tail. With tail threaded on a tapestry needle, run needle through sts on right side, bottom, and left side of rectangle, then through live sts, removing knitting needle. Pull gently on tail to gather sides of piece slightly. Wind CO tail into a ball and place in center of piece for stuffing. Pull snugly on working yarn to gather sides around stuffing. Stitch securely to fasten. Pull tail to inside of piece and trim close to surface.

FINISHING

Weave in ends. Steam helmet lightly to block.

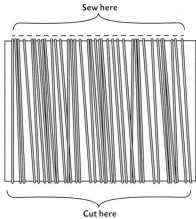

Making the Beard

Sew here

Cut here

Ears

With WS tog, sew ear linings to ears. Fold ears in half lengthwise and tack in place about ½" (1.25 cm) from fold, forming pleat. Pin ears to top of helmet, equidistant from center. Wrap MC loosely around 2 fingers 20 times for ear tuft. Tie at center and cut ends to make tassel. Wrap tassel close to top and secure strand. Trim ends evenly. Sew ear tufts in front of ears, as shown.

Muzzle

Stuff nose and sew to end of muzzle. With MC, embroider nostrils as shown. Stuff muzzle and pin to center front of helmet. Sew in place.

Eyes

With embroidery needle and MC, embroider pupils at center of eyes as shown. Wrap MC loosely around 2 fingers 26 times for eyebrow. Tie at center and cut ends. (Do not wrap as for a tassel.) Sew to back of eye with hand sewing needle and thread, spreading out strands to cover back of eye. Try on hat for eye placement. Pin and sew eyes between ears and muzzle as shown.

Beard (make 4)

Wrap MC around short end of cardboard 40 times without overlapping. With hand sewing needle and matching thread, sew strands tog with a backstitch, as shown in illustration. Cut loops

apart opposite stitching. Pin one beard piece to each side of muzzle, approx. halfway down, and sew across top along prior stitching line. Pin one beard piece to each side of muzzle, matching at center top. Sew in place along prior stitching line. Pin tongue to center front of muzzle and sew in place. Trim front beard strands to approx. 1" (2.5 cm), exposing lower tongue. Trim ear tufts, eyebrows, and beard strands as needed.

Earflap tassels (make 2)

Wrap MC around long end of cardboard 50 times. Tie at top and cut open bottom loops. Wrap top of tassel and secure strand. Trim bottom of tassel evenly. Sew tassels to points of earflaps.

SUGAR SKULL ·········

Día de los Muertos (Day of the Dead) celebrations in Mexico traditionally include treats decorated with skulls made of sugar and embellished in bright colors. Inspired by those works of edible art, this balaclava makes a fun and unusual ski mask. Sugar Skull is a simple knitted mask, embroidered with French knots and satin stitch motifs in bright yarn.

In researching the patterns, I was surprised and delighted to find many similarities between these flowers and swirls and those used in the Norwegian folk embroidery called rosemaling. Looking further, I found embroideries from Ukraine, China, and Bavaria that all reminded me of the Mexican designs. It's a small world, after all.

Yarn

 Light

Shown: 220 Superwash Sport by Cascade Yarns, 100% superwash merino wool, 1.75 oz (50 g)/ 137 yd (125 m): Black #815 (MC), 2 skeins; Aran #817 (CA), 1 skein; Pumpkin #822 (CB), 1 skein; Really Red #809 (CC), 1 skein; Dark Aqua #849 (CD), 1 skein; Raspberry #807 (CE), 1 skein; Green Apple #802 (CF), 1 skein

Needles

Size 3 (3.25 mm) 16" (40 cm) circular or size to obtain gauge

Size 3 (3.25 mm) set of dpn

Size 2 (2.75 mm) set of dpn

Notions

Stitch markers

Stitch holders

Tapestry needle

Water-soluble stabilizer (shown: Sulky Super Solvy Water Soluble Stabilizer, medium weight; item #405-01)

Embroidery needle

6" (15 cm) embroidery hoop

Silver or white permanent marker

Hand sewing needle and basting thread

Gauge

27 sts and 38 rnds = 4" (10 cm) in St st on larger needle. Take time to check gauge.

Sizes

Finished size: 19 (21¼, 22½)" (48.5 [54, 57] cm) circumference

BALACLAVA

With MC and larger circular needle, CO 128 (144, 152) sts. Pm and join for working in rnds. Work in k2, p2 rib until piece measures 2½" (6.5 cm) from CO. Knit every rnd until piece measures 6½ (7, 7½)" (16.5 [18, 19] cm) from CO.

Eye holes

K14 and place these 14 sts on holder for left eye hole.

Work back and forth over next 12 sts for eye separator as foll:

Dec row (RS): K1, ssk, knit to last 3 sts, k2tog, k1—2 sts dec'd.

Next row: Purl.

Rep last 2 rows 2 more times—6 sts. Work 2 rows in St st on these 6 sts. Work back and forth on these 6 sts as foll:

Inc row (RS): K1, M1R, knit to last st, M1L, k1—2 sts inc'd.

Next row: Purl.

Rep last 2 rows 2 more times—12 sts. Break yarn and place 12 sts on holder. With RS facing, rejoin MC at base of right eye. K14 and place these 14 sts on holder for right eye hole. Cont as foll, working back and forth in rows:

Dec row (RS): K1, ssk, knit last 3 sts of rnd, k2tog, k1—2 sts dec'd.

Next row: Purl.

Rep last 2 rows 2 more times—82 (98, 106) sts. Work 2 rows in St st.

Inc row (RS): K1, M1R, knit to last st of rnd, M1L, k1—2 sts inc'd.

Next row: Purl.

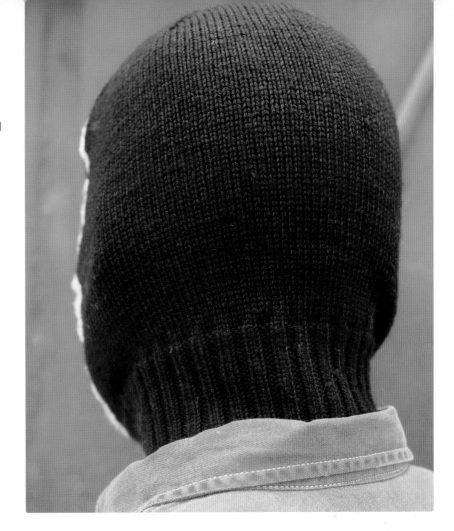

Rep last 2 rows 2 more times—88 (104, 112) sts. Knit to end of rnd. Pm for beg of rnd, CO 14 sts over left eye, k12 held sts, CO 14 sts over right eye, join and work to end of rnd—128 (144, 152) sts. Knit every rnd until piece measures 9½ (10, 10½)" (24 [25.5, 26.5] cm) from CO.

CROWN

Next rnd: K16 (18, 19), pm; rep from * to end of rnd.

Dec rnd: *Knit to 2 sts before marker, k2tog; rep from * to end of rnd—8 sts dec'd.

Next rnd: Knit.

Rep last 2 rnds 14 (16, 17) more times—8 sts. Break yarn and thread tail through rem sts. Fasten securely on WS.

(continued)

FINISHING
Eye trim

With CA, smaller dpn, and RS facing, k14 held sts, pick up and knit 14 sts along right edge of eye hole, 14 sts along top edge, and 14 sts along left edge—56 sts total. Pm and join for working in rnds. Work 3 rnds in k1, p1 rib. BO in patt.

Weave in ends. Block balaclava.

Embroidery

Photocopy and enlarge embroidery pattern (opposite) 150%. Place stabilizer over design and trace with silver or white permanent marker. Place a second sheet of stabilizer inside balaclava. Lay on a flat surface and place stabilizer sheet with pattern tracing on top of balaclava, aligning with eye openings. Pin through all 3 layers, being careful not to catch back layer of balaclava. Baste around edge of pattern with hand sewing needle and thread. Insert front of balaclava into hoop. Beg with trim around eyes, embroider with satin st and French knots in colors as shown, referring to Techniques chapter, page 123, for instructions. Move hoop as needed to complete all areas, working from center of design out. Outline teeth with MC, as shown.

Weave in ends. Remove stabilizer following manufacturer's instructions.

Tip: Superwash yarn can stretch greatly when immersed in water (as you will do to remove the water-soluble stabilizer); don't be alarmed if your balaclava seems misshapen or puckered at this stage. Be sure to let dry completely before wearing.

Embroidery Pattern

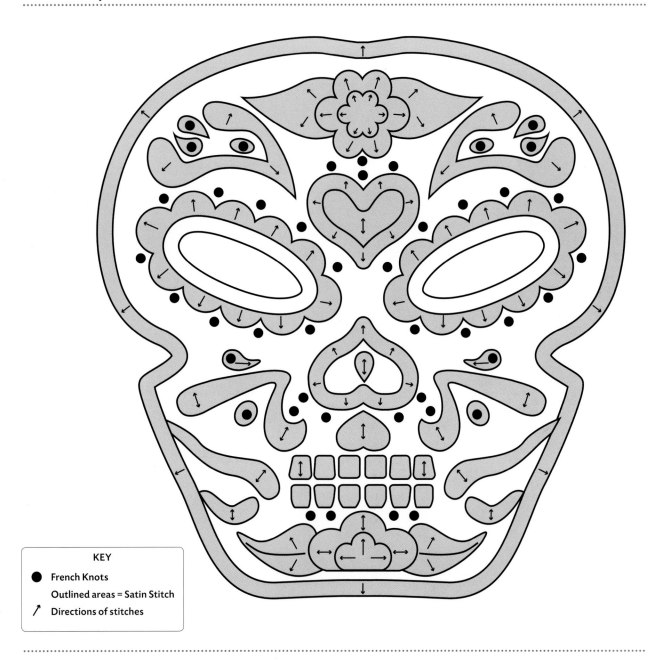

KEY

● French Knots

Outlined areas = Satin Stitch

↗ Directions of stitches

tEA PARTY

"IN THAT DIRECTION," THE CAT SAID, WAVING ITS RIGHT PAW ROUND,
"LIVES A HATTER: AND IN THAT DIRECTION," WAVING THE OTHER PAW,
"LIVES A MARCH HARE. VISIT EITHER YOU LIKE: THEY'RE BOTH MAD."

"BUT I DON'T WANT TO GO AMONG MAD PEOPLE," ALICE REMARKED.

"OH, YOU CAN'T HELP THAT," SAID THE CAT: "WE'RE ALL MAD HERE.
I'M MAD. YOU'RE MAD."

"HOW DO YOU KNOW I'M MAD?" SAID ALICE.

"YOU MUST BE," SAID THE CAT, "OR YOU WOULDN'T HAVE COME HERE."

—Through the Looking-Glass

There is nothing so elegant as a top hat. Worn to tea, or out about town, this one makes a statement, to be sure. I especially enjoyed wearing mine on Derby Day, in the USA. Change the ribbon according to the occasion or your whim—how about tartan wool for winter? And don't worry; no madness-inducing chemicals are required here. One lump, or two?

Yarn

 Medium

Shown: Classic Wool Worsted by Patons, 100% wool, 3.5 oz (100 g)/210 yd (192 m): Black #00226 (MC), 3 skeins; Winter White #00201 (CA), 1 skein; Magenta #77402 (CB), 1 skein

Needles

Size 11 (8 mm) 16" (40 cm) circular or size to obtain gauge

Size 11 (8 mm) set of dpn

Size 10 (6 mm) straight needles

Notions

Stitch markers

Removable markers

Tapestry needle

1½ yd (1.5 m) 2½" (63 mm) grosgrain ribbon (shown: May Arts #351-46)

1½ yd (1.5 m) 1½" (38 mm) grosgrain ribbon (shown: May Arts #NY-22)

2 yd (2 m) ¼" (6 mm) polyester boning

Hand sewing needle and thread

Gauge

12 sts and 16 rnds = 4" (10 cm) in St st on larger needle, before felting. Take time to check gauge.

Sizes

Finished size: 19 (21)" (48.5 [53.5] cm) circumference

Note: Measurements are approximate; sizing is easily adjusted by blocking to your preferred measurements.

Stitch Guide

S2kp2: Sl 2 sts as if to k2tog, k1, p2sso—2 sts dec'd.

HAT

Brim

With 2 strands of MC and larger circular needle, CO 96 (104) sts. Pm and join for working in rnds. Knit 1 rnd.

Next rnd: *K10 (11), k2tog; rep from * to end of rnd—88 (96) sts.

Work even until piece measures 4" (10 cm) from CO.

Next rnd: [K1, k2tog] 4 (0) times, *k2, k2tog; rep from * to last 12 (0) sts, [k1, k2tog] 4 (0) times—64 (72) sts.

Purl 1 rnd.

SIDE

Work even in St st until piece measures 7" (18 cm) from CO.

Next rnd: *K8 (9), pm; rep from * to end of rnd.

Inc rnd: *Knit to marker, M1L, sl marker; rep from * to end of rnd—8 sts inc'd.

Work even until piece measures 10" (25 cm) from CO. Rep inc rnd—80 (88) sts. Work even until piece measures 12" (30.5 cm) from CO. Rep inc rnd—88 (96) sts. Work even until piece measures 13" (33 cm) from CO. Purl 1 rnd.

CROWN

Dec rnd: *Knit to 2 sts before marker, k2tog; rep from * to end of rnd—8 sts dec'd.

Next rnd: Knit.

Rep last 2 rnds 9 (10) more times—8 sts. Break yarn and thread tail through rem sts. Fasten securely on WS.

(continued)

Tip: It may be easier to manage two strands at once if you wind two balls together before beginning. Alternatively, you can work with one strand coming from the outside and one from the inside of the same center-pull ball.

EARS

Outer ears (make 2)

With 1 strand of CA and smaller needle, CO 5 sts.

Next row (RS): P1, k3, p1.

Next row: K1, p3, k1.

Inc row (RS): P1, M1R, knit to last st, M1L, p1—2 sts inc'd.

Rep inc row every RS row once more, then every 4th row 8 times—25 sts. Work 11 rows even, ending with a WS row.

Dec row (RS): P1, ssk, knit to last 3 sts, k2tog, p1—2 sts dec'd.

Rep dec row every 4th row once more, then every RS row 7 times—7 sts. Work 1 WS row.

Dec row (RS): P1, k1, s2kp2, k1, p1—5 sts.

Work 1 WS row.

Dec row (RS): P1, s2kp2, p1—3 sts.

Work 1 WS row.

Dec row (RS): S2kp2—1 st.

Break yarn and thread tail through rem st. Fasten securely on WS.

Ear linings (make 2)

With 1 strand of CB and smaller needle, CO 3 sts.

Next row (RS): P1, k1, p1.

Next row: K1, p1, k1.

Inc row (RS): P1, M1R, knit to last st, M1L, p1—2 sts inc'd.

Rep inc row every RS row once more, then every 4th row 6 times—19 sts. Work 15 rows even, ending with a WS row.

Dec row (RS): P1, ssk, knit to last 3 sts, k2tog, p1—2 sts dec'd.

Rep dec row every 4th row 3 more times, then every RS row 3 times—5 sts. Work 1 WS row.

Dec row (RS): P1, s2kp2, p1—3 sts.

Work 1 WS row.

Dec row (RS): S2kp2—1 st.

Break yarn and thread tail through rem st. Fasten securely on WS.

FINISHING

Weave in ends. Felt all pieces (pages 120–121). Block hat to finished dimensions indicated on schematic. Block outer ears to 9" × 4" (23 × 10 cm) and ear linings to 8½" × 3" (21.5" × 7.5 cm).

Air-dry. Optional: To stiffen upper edge of hat crown, turn hat WS out and sew boning into crease, overlapping ends.

Hat band

Layer narrow ribbon on top of wide ribbon and machine sew along edges. Try on hat for fit and pin band in place at correct length. Cut band to desired length, plus 1" (2.5 cm) for seam allowance. With RS tog, sew ends of ribbon tog using ½" (1.25 cm) seam allowance. Place band on hat and tack in place by hand.

Bow

Cut a length of ribbon 15" (38 cm) long. With RS tog, sew ends of ribbon tog using ½" (1.25 cm) seam allowance. Turn RS out. Fold bow in center to form pleat and tack in place. Wrap narrow ribbon around center of pleat to form knot. Fold under raw edge and sew knot closed around bow. Tack bow in place on hat over ribbon seam.

Ears

Cut 2 pieces of boning, each ¾" (1 cm) shorter than outer ears. Pin one piece of boning to WS of each outer ear along center, with lower edge of boning even with lower edge of ear. Sew in place invisibly by hand. With WS tog, sew ear linings to outer ears. Fold lower edges of each ear tog to form a pleat and sew in place. Try on hat for ear placement and pin in place. Sew ears in place at lower edges, and tack in place about three-quarters of the way up each ear.

Blocking the Hat

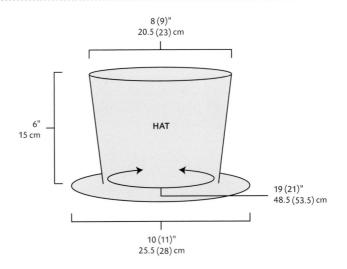

8 (9)"
20.5 (23) cm

6"
15 cm

HAT

19 (21)"
48.5 (53.5) cm

10 (11)"
25.5 (28) cm

tORTOISE

SO WHAT'S YOUR BIG FAT HURRY, ANYWAY? THE WHOLE
WIDE WORLD SEEMS TO BE IN A RACE WITH ITSELF. BUT
EVERYTHING THAT CAN BE MADE TO GO FASTER DOESN'T
NECESSARILY NEED TO.

Think about it: Do you want to get to the end of your vacation
any faster than you strictly have to? Of course not. Would you
like to have that hot bubble bath over and done with as quick
as you can? Not on your life. And what about those precious
few minutes you get each day with your family and friends? See
any need to optimize their speed and efficiency? Nope. Knitters
understand this better than most: Faster is not always better.
Make a hat to help you remember; it's okay to take it slow.

Yarn

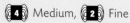 Medium, (2) Fine

Shown: Shetland Heather by Jamieson's, 100%
shetland wool, 1.75 oz (50 g)/101 yd (92 m):
Autumn #998 (MC), 2 skeins

Double Knitting by Jamieson's, 100% shetland
wool, 0.88 oz (25 g)/82 yd (75 m): Fern #249
(CA), 2 skeins; Burnt Umber #1190 (CB), 1 skein;
Mustard #425 (CC), 1 skein

Needles

Size 7 (4.5 mm) 16" (40 cm) circular or size
to obtain gauge

Size 7 (4.5 mm) set of dpn

Size 6 (4 mm) 16" (40 cm) circular

Size 3 (3.25 mm) 16" (40 cm) circular or size
to obtain gauge

Size 3 (3.25 mm) set of dpn

Notions

Stitch markers	Hand sewing needle and thread
Removable markers	Wool roving or other stuffing
Tapestry needle	Two 4 mm beads for eyes
	Pins

Gauge

20 sts and 28 rnds = 4" (10 cm) in St st with MC
on largest needle

28 sts and 36 rnds = 4" (10 cm) in St st with CA
on smallest needle

Take time to check gauge

Sizes

Finished size: 17½ (19¼, 22½)" (44.5 [49, 57] cm)
circumference

Stitch Guide

S2kp2: Sl 2 sts as if to k2tog, k1, p2sso—2 sts dec'd.

HAT

Side

With MC and middle-size circular needle, CO 88 (96, 112) sts. Pm and join for working in rnds. Work in k1, p1 rib until piece measures ¾" (2 cm) from CO. Change to largest circular needle. Knit every rnd until piece measures 4 (4½, 5)" (10 [11.5, 12.5] cm) from CO.

Crown

Next rnd: *K11 (12, 14), pm; rep from * to end of rnd.

Dec rnd: *Knit to 2 sts before marker, k2tog; rep from * to end of rnd—8 sts dec'd.

Next rnd: Knit.

Rep last 2 rnds 9 (10, 12) more times—8 sts. Break yarn and thread tail through rem sts. Fasten securely on WS.

SHELL HEXAGONS (make 7)

With CA and smallest dpn, CO 54 sts. Distribute sts evenly onto 3 dpn, pm, and join for working in rnds.

Rnd 1: Purl.

Rnd 2: *K6, s2kp2; rep from * to end of rnd—42 sts.

Rnd 3: Knit, sl first st of each dpn to previous needle after knitting it.

Change to CB.

Rnd 4: *K4, s2kp2; rep from * to end of rnd—30 sts.

Rnd 5: Knit, sl first st of each dpn to previous needle after knitting it.

Rnd 6: *K2, s2kp2; rep from * to end of rnd—18 sts.

Change to CC.

Rnd 7: Knit, sl first st of each dpn to previous needle after knitting it.

Rnd 8: *S2kp2; rep from * to end of rnd—6 sts.

Rnd 9: Knit.

Break yarn and thread tail through rem sts. Fasten securely on WS. Arrange hexagons so there is 1 in center and 6 around edges. With CA, sew hexagons tog.

SHELL TRIANGLES (make 6)

With CA and smallest needle, CO 19 sts.

Row 1 (RS): Ssk, k15, k2tog—17 sts.

Row 2 (WS): P2tog, p13, ssp—15 sts.

Row 3: Ssk, k11, k2tog—13 sts.

Change to CB.

Row 4: P2tog, p9, ssp—11 sts.

Row 5: Ssk, k7, k2tog—9 sts.

Row 6: P2tog, p5, ssp—7 sts.

Change to CC.

Row 7: Ssk, k3, k2tog—5 sts.

Row 8: P2tog, p1, ssp—3 sts.

Row 9: S2kp2—1 st.

Break yarn and thread tail through rem st. Fasten securely on WS. Arrange triangles in notches between hexagons. With CA, sew triangles to hexagons.

(continued)

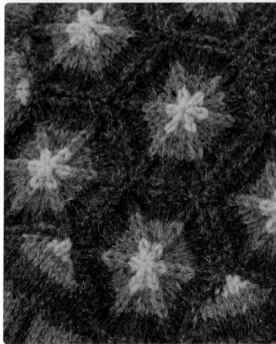

SHELL BORDER

With CA, smallest circular needle, and RS facing, pick up and knit 168 sts around edge of shell. Pm and join for working in rnds. Purl 1 rnd.

Next 3 rnds: *K2 with CA, k6 with CB; rep from * to end of rnd.

Inc rnd: *K2 with CA, k3 with CB, M1, k3 with CB; rep from * to end of rnd—189 sts.

Next 2 rnds: *K2 with CA, k7 with CB; rep from * to end of rnd.

Change to CA. Knit 3 rnds. Purl 1 rnd.

Next rnd: *K27, pm; rep from * to end of rnd.

Change to CC.

Dec rnd: *Knit to 2 sts before marker, k2tog; rep from * to end of rnd—7 sts dec'd.

Next rnd: Knit.

Rep last 2 rnds 10 more times—112 sts. BO.

HEAD

With CA, smallest dpn, and using Judy's magic CO (page 124) or other toe-up method, CO 8 sts—4 sts on each of 2 dpn. Pm and join for working in rnds.

Next rnd: K4, pm, k4.

Inc rnd: *K1, M1R, knit to 1 st before marker, M1L, k1; rep from * once more—4 sts inc'd.

Next rnd: Knit.

Rep last 2 rnds 3 more times—24 sts. Knit 8 rnds. Stuff head.

Dec rnd: *K2, k2tog; rep from * to end of rnd—18 sts.

Knit 3 rnds.

Dec rnd: *K1, k2tog; rep from * to end of rnd—12 sts.

Knit 6 rnds. BO.

LEGS (make 4)

With CA and smallest dpn, CO 12 sts. Pm and join for working in rnds. Knit every rnd until piece measures 2" (5 cm) from CO.

Next rnd: *P3, using the knitted method, CO 3 sts, BO 3 sts; rep from * to end of rnd—12 sts.

Knit 1 rnd.

Next rnd: *K2tog; rep from * to end of rnd—6 sts.

Break yarn and thread tail through rem sts. Fasten securely on WS.

TAIL

With CA and smallest dpn, CO 12 sts. Pm and join for working in rnds. Knit every rnd until piece measures 1" (2.5 cm) from CO.

Next rnd: *K2, k2tog; rep from * to end of rnd—9 sts.

Knit 3 rnds.

Next rnd: *K1, k2tog; rep from * to end of rnd—6 sts.

Knit 3 rnds.

Next rnd: *K2tog; rep from * to end of rnd—3 sts.

Knit 3 rnds. Break yarn and thread tail through rem sts. Fasten securely on WS.

FINISHING

Weave in ends. Block hat. Stuff neck, legs, and tail. Stuff shell loosely. Pin shell in place at top of hat and sew in place along shell BO with hand sewing needle and thread. Pin head to underside of shell at center front of hat. Sew in place, closing neck opening. Tack shell to hat at each side of head. Attach legs and tail as for head. Thread tapestry needle with CB and embroider mouth and eyes as shown. Sew beads in place with hand sewing needle and thread.

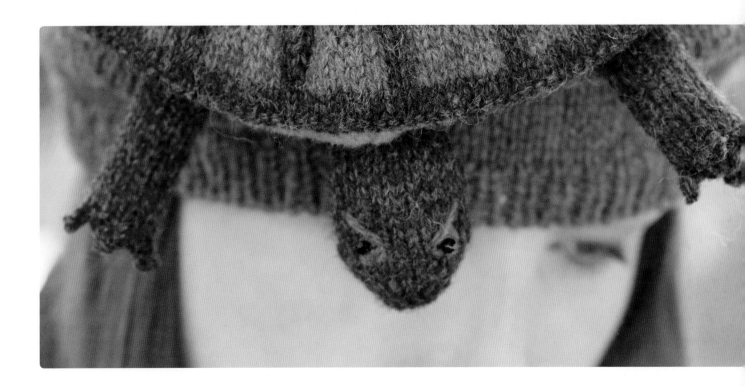

tECHNIQUES

Many of the hats in this collection include elements of soft sculpture. Because the nature of knitted fabric is to be soft and fluid, there are a few steps we need to take to help the sculptural elements stand out (or up) properly.

GAUGE

In almost every case, the knitted fabric you make for these hats will be firmer than that suggested by the yarn manufacturer. For this reason, you'll need to be especially careful when making yarn substitutions. To successfully substitute yarns, check the CYCA symbol number listed at the beginning of each pattern, and make sure the yarn you are considering has the same symbol. This way you can tell whether you are choosing a comparable weight of yarn, regardless of the gauge(s) I have recommended for the project.

For example, Mercury's helmet is made from #4 (medium) yarn, which has a stated gauge of 20 stitches and 26 rows over 4" (10.2 cm). For the project, though, I chose to work the same yarn at a much smaller gauge for the wings (24 stitches and 32 rows in 4" [10.2 cm] on a size 4 needle) in order to give them enough body.

In other words, pay attention to the manufacturer's yarn weight when choosing your yarns, then the gauge given in the pattern when you knit.

STUFFING

Sometimes making the knitting firmer isn't enough. Many of the elements in the patterns call for you to make separate pieces that are filled with stuffing. The stuffing called for is usually either wool roving, available wherever spinning supplies are sold, or for very small pieces, the same yarn they are knitted from. Stuffing a knitted piece with its own yarn has the advantage that you can fill the piece quite firmly without the stuffing showing through the knitted fabric. Polyester, cotton, or blended batting could also be used, but I prefer roving because of its ability to resist forming clumps inside small pieces.

STIFFENERS

In places where stuffing a piece would make it too bulky, or where an element is actually resisting gravity, I've used internal and external armatures for support. A weightless and nearly invisible way to support knitted fabric is with monofilament fishing line. You can find 100-lb test monofilament where fishing equipment is sold. To finish the ends of monofilament, I suggest jewelry crimp tubes, which are available at craft supply stores.

The firmest stiffener used in the collection is polyester boning. This is the exact same boning used in evening wear and lingerie, and can be found in the notions department of your fabric store. Because boning is usually either black or white, it needs to be concealed in order to avoid detracting from the design. The projects that call for boning give instructions for how to do so.

FELTING

Some of the projects in this collection call for you to knit them in a larger-than-usual size and then felt them. Felted knits are much stiffer and more substantial, giving your hats and decorative elements a sturdy backbone all their own.

There are many ways to felt your knitting, but they all require the same basic elements: water, heat, and agitation. Some pieces, like swatches and small details, are easier to felt by hand. Others are more manageable using a washing machine, due to their size or the yarn you're using. Every yarn will felt differently, so take your time and check on your progress as often as is practical. Remember: Only untreated (non-superwash) yarn will felt. Any other manmade fibers added to the mix will keep your project from succeeding, so check your labels carefully, and if in doubt, get the exact same yarn specified in the pattern.

By Hand

Fill a bucket, sink, or bathtub with enough piping hot water to cover your piece, with room to swish it around aggressively. Add a squirt of dishwashing liquid or laundry detergent to remove any residual spinning oils and dirt from the yarn. Wearing rubber gloves will protect your

hands as well as provide a little extra traction against the project, particularly if the gloves have textured ridges on the palms. Add your project to the felting bath and let it sit for 20 or 30 minutes to allow the water to penetrate the fibers; this makes the felting go much more quickly. Then scrub, squish, smash, and generally throttle it in the hot water. The length of time you will need to continue this part varies greatly with each yarn type, so check your progress often by squeezing the water out of the piece and evaluating the fabric. Experiment with household utensils, like potato mashers, rubber plungers, and the like, particularly if your hands get tired. Add more hot water and detergent when the bath starts to cool. You can also give your project a "shock" rinse in cold water between baths to further the process.

By Machine

You may have heard that it is not possible to felt your knitting in a front-loading washing machine. Although top-loading machines are generally faster, rest assured that they aren't the only way. Front loaders are gentler, and so may take longer, but they will get the job done. To begin, choose the hottest, shortest cycle on your machine. You may need to repeat the cycle, or choose a longer one, but it's safer to work in stages to avoid over-felting.

Place your project into a mesh laundry bag. This is to protect your machine from choking on loose fibers, should the yarn shed too much, and also to keep any small parts from getting lost. Add a pair of jeans or two, and a few clean tennis balls. Washable athletic shoes are also great for felting, particularly if they have rough soles; just be sure to remove the laces first. Use regular laundry detergent, but don't add liquid fabric softener. Start the machine and let the magic begin. After the machine has filled with water, stop the cycle and let the project sit for 20 or 30 minutes to allow the water to penetrate the fibers; this makes the felting go much more quickly. After resuming the cycle, check your project from time to time, if your washer allows (it's hard to stop a front-loader mid-cycle), to evaluate the felting.

Whether you felt by hand or machine, you'll be able to tell the felting is complete when your piece matches the finished dimensions indicated in the pattern (or a bit smaller—you can always stretch felted items somewhat, but if they're too big, you can only do more felting). Generally speaking, the knitted stitches should no longer be defined, the surface of the fabric should have a fuzzy "halo," and the fabric should be smooth and even when you are done. If any of these properties is absent, but the size is correct, stop felting. If all these characteristics are present but the piece is still too large, felt some more.

EMBROIDERY

All of the embroidery called for in this book is done using the same yarn as the rest of the project. When embroidering onto knitted fabric, remember to use a sharp-pointed embroidery needle, rather than the blunt-tipped tapestry needle you'd choose to weave in ends. To get the embroidery stitches to fall precisely where you want them, it's necessary to pierce through the plies of the yarn, which can only be done with a sharp needle.

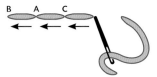

Backstitch

Work individual stitches from right to left. Come up at A, take a small backward stitch, go down at B, and emerge at C. Always move the needle forward under the fabric and come up one stitch length ahead, ready to take another stitch. Keep the stitch lengths even.

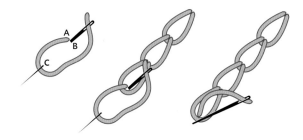

Chain Stitch

Come up at A and form a loop. Go down at B, as close to A as possible, but not into it. Emerge at C, bringing the needle tip over the thread. Repeat this stitch to make a chain.

Blocking Felt

Once your pieces are felted, you'll need to stretch, mold, and manipulate them into shape. Bowls, flowerpots, paint cans, and vases can all make excellent hat forms. Look carefully around your house for objects the right size and shape to block your felting. Use rolled towels, sewing pins, and even duct tape to get your hat form to just the right size and shape. Place your hat over its form, stretching and smoothing it into shape. Pin flat pieces down on an ironing or blocking board. This is the time to apply steam from your iron if you need to manipulate the felt even more. Let the pieces air-dry completely before final finishing. If you aren't happy with the final result after blocking, don't hesitate to wet the piece again and start over. Unlike regular knitting, felted knits can withstand aggressive blocking, and even look better for it.

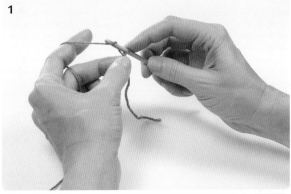

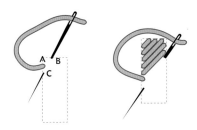

Satin Stitch

Come up at A and go down at B, making a straight stitch the desired length, then emerge at C. Continue working straight stitches close together without overlapping, keeping the edge of the design even and defined.

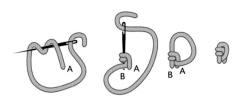

French Knot

Come up at A and wrap the yarn twice around the needle. Holding thread taught, go down at B as close to A as possible, but not into it. Hold the knot in place until the needle and yarn are pulled all the way through.

CROCHET CHAIN

Make a slip knot and place on crochet hook.

1. Bring yarn over hook from back to front and grab it with hook.

2. Draw hooked yarn through slip knot and onto hook—1 chain stitch is complete.

Repeat steps 1 and 2, pulling hooked yarn through new loop on hook, until chain reaches desired length. Break yarn and pull tail through last stitch.

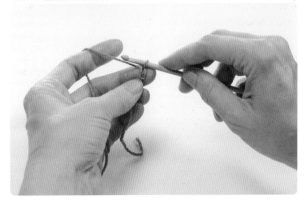

PROVISIONAL CAST ON

There are many kinds of provisional cast ons. This one is easy to remove. Choose a smooth, durable waste yarn (cotton works well) and any medium-size crochet hook.

1. With waste yarn and crochet hook, make a slip knot, then chain 2 or 3 stitches. Hold the hook in your right hand and a knitting needle in your left. *With the crochet hook above the needle and the working yarn below it, wrap the yarn around the hook.

2. Pull the yarn through the loop on the hook.

3. Bring the working yarn to the back, under the needle.

4. Repeat from *, until you have made the required number of stitches. Chain 2 or 3 stitches with the crochet hook and break waste yarn.

5. Knit 1 row with working yarn to complete the cast on. Then continue the knitting pattern.

6. To remove waste yarn, loosen end of chain and pull through the end of the last chain stitch. Gently pull on the tail of the waste yarn to release one live knitting stitch at a time, placing on needle.

JUDY'S MAGIC CAST ON

(Visit http://knitty.com/ISSUEspring06/FEATmagiccaston. html for detailed instructions and photos.)

Conceived for use in toe-up sock knitting, this cast on is useful for pieces that are worked from a closed end to an open one. Use two double-pointed needles to work the cast on.

1. Make a slip knot and place the loop around one needle. This is the first stitch.

2. Hold both needles parallel in your right hand, the needle with the slip knot on top. The upper needle is #2 and the lower needle is #1.

3. In your left hand, hold yarn so the tail goes over your index finger and working end goes over your thumb.

4. Bring the tip of needle #1 over the strand of yarn on your finger, around and under the yarn, and back up, making a loop around needle #1, pulling yarn snug— 1 stitch on needle #1.

5. Bring needle #2 over the yarn tail on your thumb, around and under the yarn and back up, making a loop around needle #2, pulling yarn snug—2 stitches on needle #2.

Top strand always wraps around lower needle (#1); bottom strand always wraps around upper needle (#2).

Repeat steps 4 and 5 until the desired number of stitches is cast on, ending with step 4. To work the first round, rotate the needles so that #1 is on top, and begin knitting. When all the stitches from needle #1 have been worked, you will see a row of stitches appear between the two needles. Continue knitting across needle #2, working the stitches through the back loop so that they aren't twisted. Incorporate additional double-pointed needles as piece grows.

THREE-NEEDLE BIND OFF

This technique joins any two sets of live stitches into a secure and bulk-free seam. It only works when the two pieces contain the exact same number of stitches to be joined.

Place one set of live stitches onto each of two needles. Hold the pieces to be joined in your left hand with right sides together. (See photos below.)

1. With your right hand, insert a third needle through the first stitch on each needle (a). Wrap the working yarn, then pull the new stitch through both the old ones, slipping them off their needles (b).

2. Work the next stitches from each needle together, then pass the first stitch on the right needle over the second to bind off.

Repeat step 2 until all stitches from both pieces are worked. Break working yarn and pull tail through last loop.

SHORT ROWS

When working short rows, you shape the knitting by working partway through a row, then turning the work and going back the other way. There are many ways to work short rows. This "wrap and turn" method involves two stages. The first is wrapping and turning, in which you wrap the working yarn around a stitch at the turning point to avoid leaving a hole in the work. The second stage is completed the next time that stitch is worked, when you pick up the wrap and work it together with a live stitch to hide it.

Wrap and Turn

1. Work the row for the specified number of stitches, either knitting or purling.

2. Slip the next stitch purlwise.

3. Bring yarn between the needles to the other side of the work and slip the same stitch to the left-hand needle.

4. Turn. Purl or knit the next stitch as specified.

Pick up Wraps

To knit a wrapped stitch, insert needle from bottom to top, front to back, under wrap, then knitwise into wrapped stitch. Knit wrap and stitch together.

To purl a wrapped stitch, insert needle from bottom to top, back to front, under wrap, then purlwise into wrapped stitch. Purl wrap and stitch together.

1a

1b

2

ABBREVIATIONS

[ ]	work instructions between brackets as many times as directed
*	repeat instructions following the asterisk as indicated
"	inches
approx	approximately
beg	begin(ning)
BO	bind off
CA	color A
CB	color B
CC	color C or contrasting color
cm	centimeter(s)
CO	cast on
cont	continue
dec	decrease(s)(ing)
dpn	double-pointed needle(s)
foll	following
g	gram
inc	increase(s)(ing)
k	knit
kwise	knitwise
k2tog	knit two stitches together
LH	left hand
m	meter(s)
MC	main color
M1L	make one left
M1R	make one right
oz	ounce(s)

p	purl
patt(s)	pattern(s)
pm	place marker
prev	previous
pwise	purlwise
p2sso	pass two slipped stitches over
p2tog	purl two stitches together
rem	remain(s)(ing)
rep	repeat(s)
rev St st	reverse stockinette stitch
RH	right hand
rnd(s)	round(s)
RS	right side
sl	slip
sl1p	slip one stitch purlwise
ssk	[slip one stitch knitwise] two times, work these two stitches together
ssp	[slip one stitch knitwise] two times, transfer two stitches to left needle, purl two stitches together through back loops
st(s)	stitch(es)
St st	stockinette stitch
tbl	through back loop
tog	together
WS	wrong side
yd(s)	yard(s)
yo	yarn over

RESOURCES

Patons Yarns
320 Livingstone Ave. South, Box 40
Listowel, ON, Canada N4W 3H3
www.yarnspirations.com/patons

Kauni / RYN Yarn
PO Box 170561
Glendale, WI 53217
www.rynyarn.com

Abstract Fiber
3673 SE Martins Street
Portland, OR 97202
www.abstractfiber.com

Freia Handpaints
6023 Christie Avenue
Emeryville, CA 94608
www.freiafibers.com

Cascade Yarns
1224 Andover Park E,
Tukwila, WA 98188
http://cascadeyarns.com

Blue Moon Fiber Arts
56587 Mollenhour Road
Scappoose, OR 97056
www.bluemoonfiberarts.com

Simply Shetland
18375 Olympic Avenue South
Seattle, WA 97188
http://simplyshetland.net

Lion Brand Yarns
34 West 15th Street
New York, NY 10011
http://lionbrand.com

Madeline Tosh
7515 Benbrook Parkway
Benbrook, TX 76126
http://madelinetosh.com